READING THE WORLD

THROUGH THE LIVING WORD

FRANCISCAN LECTIO

FR. DAN RILEY, OFM

WITH STEPHEN COPELAND

San Damiano Books
PARACLETE PRESS

2022 First and Second Printing

Franciscan Lectio: Reading the World through the Living Word

Copyright © 2022 by The Order of Friars Minor of the Province of the Most Holy Name and Stephen Copeland

Drawings by Daniel Riley, OFM. Drawing on page 215 by Dan Wintermantle, given to Dan Riley.

ISBN 978-1-64060-528-2

Library of Congress Cataloging-in-Publication Data

Names: Riley, Daniel, 1943- author. | Copeland, Stephen (Sports writer), author.
Title: Franciscan lectio : reading the world through the living word /
    Daniel Riley, OFM, with Stephen Copeland.
Description: Brewster, Massachusetts : Paraclete Press, [2022] | Includes
    bibliographical references. | Summary: "A book for Christians who long
    to see the world more beautifully and deeply and become more attentive
    and present"-- Provided by publisher.
Identifiers: LCCN 2022015939 (print) | LCCN 2022015940 (ebook) | ISBN
    9781640605282 (trade paperback) | ISBN 9781640605299 (epub) | ISBN
    9781640605305 (pdf)
Subjects: LCSH: Bible--Devotional use. | Prayer--Catholic Church. | BISAC:
    RELIGION / Prayer | RELIGION / Christian Living / Personal Growth
Classification: LCC BS617.8 .R55 2022 (print) | LCC BS617.8 (ebook) | DDC
    220.6--dc23/eng/20220517
LC record available at https://lccn.loc.gov/2022015939
LC ebook record available at https://lccn.loc.gov/2022015940

10 9 8 7 6 5 4 3 2

Published by Paraclete Press
Brewster, Massachusetts
www.paracletepress.com

Printed in the United States of America

CONTENTS

A NOTE TO THE READER
7

INTRODUCTION
13

PART I
GAZE
READING THE WORD ON THE FACE OF CREATION
19

PART II
CONSIDER
RUMINATING ON THE WORD
103

PART III
CONTEMPLATE
TRANSFORMATION THROUGH THE WORD
147

PART IV
IMITATE
TAKING THE WORD INTO THE WORLD
179

ACKNOWLEDGMENTS
217

"RECIPES" FOR LECTIO
219

OTHER RECOMMENDED RESOURCES
223

NOTES
229

To

My mother, Jane Frances (Dalton);
My father, James "Jake" Riley;
My brother Jim, now deceased;
My younger brother, Denny;
and
My two sisters, Patty and Ellen.

"Sometimes we go on a search and do not know what we are looking for until we come again to our beginning."
—ROBERT LAX

A NOTE TO THE READER

*H*ave you ever tried running? Running takes us *outside* and *into* a world around us, but it doesn't ask for equipment—good running shoes and athletic clothes. Or how about practicing yoga? All you need is a mat . . . and a good teacher.

Lectio is its own practice. It is an opening to what reading means—to the meaning of our own reading of the world, reality, sacred texts, and everything that might open the eye of our heart. This intimate, ancient way of reading has been neglected in our age. Let us begin to call it Franciscan Lectio.

This might seem like strange and new territory. When Jesus sent his friends out into the world, he told them, "Take nothing for your journey." They learned more about what they were to do the more they committed themselves to his simple call. *They discovered all that they needed along the way.*

Like running, like yoga, like the early call of the apostles, all that we need in Lectio will be found along the way.

Irish philosopher and poet John O'Donohue, who died in 2008, wrote, "I would love to live like a river flows, carried by the surprise of its own unfolding." As you enter into this "river" it might feel unfamiliar or even unnerving—the uncertainty of not knowing where the bottom might be or whether there are other creatures lurking around your legs. Yet this is already the world in which we live—a world we are within and a world that is within us. Our imaginations and soulfulness come alive, as we open ourselves to *see* and to *read* with, what St. Bonaventure would say in interpreting Ephesians, "the eyes of our hearts."

We are guides to one another in our silence, stillness, and joy in exploring that which is both ancient and new to us. We are in the river's flow together. Though we have always been in Christ, we begin to experience that we are truly made new again and again. Franciscan Lectio seeks, as T. S. Eliot wrote, to "arrive where we started and know the place for the first time."

This humble book arises from some of my own personal stories and experiences: my longing to listen and learn *from* God *within* God's world, to come to know who I am before God, and to come to know who we are as God's people. You, too, might find that this simple quest inspires you to ask a common question: "Lord, what would you have me do?" In Lectio, we are invited into the simplicity of an open heart and mind, which might begin with a sacred text but then spirals out, opening us to seeing and listening to other creatures and the rest of the world as revelatory. Like anything rooted in mysticism, it is this "subjectivity," beautiful openness, and infinite depth of Franciscan Lectio that makes it difficult, at times, to ascribe to words this practice without coming across as directive.

You should know that this is not a how-to book. This is an interpretive book, not a research document. Francis is an aesthetic and imaginal saint who, early on, walked into the world and invited us to do some magical thinking. Lectio, I believe, invites us to actively engage in vernacular theology.[1] We flow without obsessing over our destination. We "read" what is within us and around us without needing to commodify what we have learned. My goal in writing this book is not to give you the answer; rather, it is to inspire you to ask the question; to walk in unknowing, the forgotten, and to *re-cogito*—to come to know again. Though each of the four parts of this book has a heading and subheading, I do not seek to pin down their meaning. I invite you now to not only read the words in this book but in between the lines as well, and to take time with the art I've included from my own journeying without any hurry to flip to the next page. I invite you to explore your own imagination; to gaze, consider, contemplate, and imitate what each section might mean to *you* in the context of the theme. All of this is an open-ended vernacular theology that Francis pursued and Clare practiced.

Author Gerald May calls this the "power of slowing." In the worlds of culinary science, slow cooking, psychiatry, recovery, and spirituality, there have been interesting notations about the blessing of slowing. As I write this book, I pray that you and I receive the gift of slowing: to read it as you wish, no more quickly than your heart would take you.

Some of what I write in these coming pages might not make sense at first or seem rationally as if I am talking in circles; that is, until you experience Franciscan Lectio for yourself and understand that it's actually a lively sphere that spirals out as nature does. You might think of a seed with its taproot going *down* and its new shoot going *up* and winding through the soil *out* of the sun. This is the emergence of our lives as we are drawn to the Christ, the Cosmic One who is the light of the nations and the light for our own hearts. We are, in Lectio, involved in this ancient reading of life coming to be. As Christians we believe this spherical journey is the Cosmic Christ. We, in Christ, rise up from sheer nothingness into the fullness and wholeness of God, who is beyond our understanding. One might say that's a big leap. Yes, it is. That's why we take our time in our running shoes or on our yoga mat, now moving with the "power of slowing," disciplining ourselves to a quiet journey that will ask us to rest along the way.

This book is like a Responsorial Psalm—a place between two large readings of life, be it Scripture or silence, much like the rest of the created order. The response is repeated as we go deeper into a psalm. It's also why my default language is mystical and symbolic. The Word is not only read in words. Sometimes it's not read in words at all, but in everything else, even in terribly disturbing moments. Going up is also going down. I've included poetry, art, the integrative work of philosophers like Ken Wilber (who takes us outside the structure of religion), and other contemplative outlets throughout each chapter. My goal in writing is not to control your Lectio practice! Rather, I hope that it inspires your imagination so that you *lose control* of your Lectio practice in your encounter with the Christ Mystery, who transforms us in unfathomable ways. You might find this new way of reading inspires your imagination, which indeed is a gift we have within the virtue of hope.

Maybe you're wondering as you begin or continue this journey, "What do I need to learn to do Lectio?" When I began running a long time ago, I asked friends about the best shoes and local paths or tracks to train on. It was striking how often they indicated that shoes were most important. As we begin, may you find shoes that fit you well. Paths and tracks? That is up to you and your own felt experience, perhaps determined by whether you are running on your own or with others. Many of us have a habit of being weighed down by the accoutrements of its practice when we begin something, thinking we need a lot to get on with it. The wonderful thing about Lectio is that all you need are "shoes," which is to say an open heart and mind as you engage sacred Scriptures, the texts of your life, and the first text Bonaventure tells us about: Creation around and within us. The path will unfold, circle, and spiral out in many ways.

Welcome to *Franciscan Lectio*. Let it be enjoyable. Francis is a saint of joy. His spirit moved him to dance on the face of the earth, even when he was encountering human misery and the pain of others. He helped them find a road to joy. Jesus's early followers sometimes wondered, "Lord, where do you stay?" and Jesus simply said, "Come and see." You and I are invited in Lectio to step beyond where we have been and follow the One who truly has stayed among us, who is present here and now, and bidding us to use all of our senses says, "Come and see."

"Place your mind before the mirror of eternity . . ."
—ST. CLARE OF ASSISI

"In the beginning was the Word and the Word was with God and the Word was God. God was in the beginning, he was in the beginning with God. All things came to be through him, and without him nothing came to be."
—JOHN 1:1-3

"Come; everything is now ready."
—LUKE 14:17

"You . . . will set my feet in a free and open space."
—PSALM 31:9

INTRODUCTION

I grew up in a public school family, which in those days was quite different from a Catholic school family. We were practicing Catholics, and our prayers were rich and full around our beds at night. Some of my friends were already beginning to feel confined by faith practices, and I understand now why they were experiencing discomfort and distance from religion.

As a public school kid, I went to "release time" religious education. A bus waited for us as we trailed out of the school building, then took us to the Catholic grammar school a mile and a half away. During a visit to the church one day, I remember Father O'Malley meeting us at the bus, juggling snowballs. But, most often, I sensed a taught separation between me and the sacred. During another visit, I remember our teacher telling us not to enter the sanctuary in the church and instructing us not to touch any of the vessels on the altar, which we needed to stay far from. Of course, then, there was a sturdy communion rail that would make it difficult to go further. All this seemed to heighten the sense that God was distant and untouchable, as if we were to be as well. There was an apparent divide between being human and being holy.

It wasn't until I attended St. Bonaventure University that the veil was lifted.

Upon arriving on campus, I remember being given a list of books to buy at the bookstore. I bought a pile without paying much attention to their contents, tossed them in a bag, and carried them back to Devereux Hall. There, I took each book out slowly, looking at it and placing each one on the other on my desk. The last one I removed from my bag was a Bible for theology class. I carefully picked it up, then put it in place on top of the others. It sat there, showing itself to me.

In the Roman Catholic tradition, the monstrance is brought out and placed, often on the altar or sacred alcove. I would have seen this numerous times. But now I was sitting immediately before the text, with full accessibility to this sacred book, what I was already beginning to believe to be God's presence. I had an inkling this was not first about instruction but about presence. I sat there in awe. It was as if I had a monstrance in our dorm room.

To have the Bible within a foot and a half of my face and know that I was able to open it myself, not needing someone else to open it for me, was one of the most powerful moments of my early life. There was no divide. A lifted veil. I lifted it up and opened its pages, as if I was entering a new land. This was much different from the structure of religion. Some might call it, a word used now, transformational. We will call it Lectio Divina.

An ancient tradition dating back to the third century, Lectio Divina is a practice that arose out of the desert from people determined to become more grounded in the radicalness and richness of gospel living. Some whom we now know by name and their practices left the cities of Egypt and entered the desert for solitude so that they would experience *metanoia*—rooted in the Word and a change of heart—in the dazzling sun of the desert, the earth, and a world beyond urban life. They sought to discover renewed focus and spiritual insight in experiencing God's presence deep within them and around them. They deepened their focus through reading, memorizing and meditating, praying, and contemplating the Holy Scriptures—eventually called Lectio Divina.

That time, not unlike our own, called out for reformation. The Desert Fathers and Mothers realized that authentic spirituality needed to move from the inside out, not from the outside in, and move from a society that was materialistic. They realized that the Word became flesh, moving from the inside out, which revolutionized their spiritual practice. "The kingdom of God is within you. The reign of God is at hand."[2] Simple ways of eremitical life in the desert and the practice of Lectio Divina shaped their way of life enough that monasticism began to form, incorporating this beautiful practice. It still does.

Over time Lectio Divina seemed to be reserved for monastics, much like contemplation. It revolved around the reading of a sacred text. Franciscan Lectio breaks open both of these notions and connects it back to the expansiveness and openness found in our sacred Scriptures, as well as the perennial wisdom and creation in which human life arose. Silence, solitude, simplicity, and service, as we will discuss later, were natural "sisters" of Lady Poverty and Lady Wisdom, practiced in different cultures and mystical traditions. Lectio is not restricted to monasteries or monks or "the religious" or even solely to sacred texts, but is instead an activity "in the sphere of love"—God's presence—that is *holy and whole* everywhere. It is time for what was once held in monasteries, friaries, and churches to now spill out into the homes and public spaces of our world. It's time for what was once reserved for Bible reading to now also spill out into Creation, the incarnate Word. We are to take it in, where and as it is.

The "school" I come from—the Franciscan way—found most of its classrooms and books in marketplaces and in the faces of the poor; on the hillsides in mountain seclusion and in the eyes of lepers; in big cities, small towns, and universities; in sacred spaces and everyday places. Whether it was one person, one place, or one moment, the Franciscan disposition is that the reign of God is always at hand; the richness of God's glory is present here and everywhere. Each creature is a vestige of God's creative action and an expression of God's loving Word. This is the blessing of Franciscan Lectio. It is truly panoramic at a time when anxiety narrows us. The habits or patterns integrated into a way of life that we see in the way of Francis and Clare and their followers show us that they ran *into* life, inspiring us to do the same. Lectio is about reading or focusing or listening long enough and deeply enough so that beauty, depth, and connectivity emerge; peace and freedom inspire action and service.

St. Bonaventure describes justice as "the returning to its original beauty that which has been deformed." Franciscan Lectio inspires us to see original beauty more clearly and then to live out of that truth more naturally over time. I think that true freedom flows out of our rootedness in beauty.

Francis of Assisi walked in the world as if he were a gardener attending his great garden, plant by plant, amazed by everything that not only broke through the surface like the rising flowers but also all that was still in the dirt, yet to emerge. Though hidden, it was already there. Though many elements, it was always one garden. God's face, Francis believed, shone from within all that was created. Francis was a wanderer, a hermit preacher, and a minstrel of God. He was God's own juggler, juggling the wonder of the Word in the world. He was a person trying to find his way in the world, and I wonder if this is part of his hidden attraction.

At the end of Francis's life, he continued to tire his brothers out with new dreams, saying, "Let us begin now because up to now we've done almost nothing." Francis was reading and learning about God everywhere, beyond the church or the classroom, and responding to the Word as it was alive in everything. Francis realized that the world he was in held meaning in a different way.

Holiness and wholeness.

Simplicity and abundance.

Community and person.

Francis, a saint of peace, read the world and all of creation as a place where things converged in conversation for the renewal of his heart, the renewal of his brothers and sisters, the renewal of the earth upon which he walked, and the renewal of the broken world and church where he prayed and worshiped.[3]

Word and world—indeed this is our home, and we are finding ways to choose to live here together with one another. We need to pick up the Bible and at the same time our world, holding them and letting them hold us, tenderly and gently opening and beginning to page through them, but only as they offer themselves to us. We need to look everyone and everything in the face and be amazed at the face of God looking back at us.

A close friend and follower of Francis of Assisi, St. Clare, wrote to a woman named Agnes in Prague in four beautiful letters. In one letter she instructs Agnes to place herself before the mirror of eternity. I invite us all to do that now as we open ourselves to Lectio Divina. I believe that our doxology would invite us to do the same thing, as we recognize that "as it was in the beginning is now and ever shall be." In other words, there is an absolutely amazing *now* about eternity.

Have you ever looked through a telescope and seen things that are distant suddenly brought into your presence? Perhaps it made you realize that all of what is there is already here. The spiritual truth is that, in Christ, in the Word, we are born into an inheritance that has been—and will be forever—God's own reign. We are born to be one with all of creation in some profound way. It is the intimacy of the immensity of God.

It is "all in all."

"It is already now."

Franciscan Lectio is a practice in which you begin to actualize your connectedness with everything—your inherent and inherited union with the Divine. Religion has, at times, unfortunately tried to control a person's journey. Lectio is a vast and singular doorway with a simple but necessary discipline. When we enter, whether through a leaf, a conversation with a friend, a verse from St. Paul's letters, or a deep sadness, there is a unique openness to meaning, to understanding. Logic is making sense out of something; but in *logos*—the Word of God—what we have is the One who makes sense, the one who makes meaning. Our world is caught up in the logical order of things, but my hope is that our intellects are a springboard for going into *logos*. As most mystics know, authentic experience disturbs our ordering and we become somewhat disordered.

Eventually a new light comes on as we are brought into unity. We open our hearts to the conversion that is part of the habit and practice of Lectio—a conversion through reading the sacred cosmos: the Christ that is in everyone and every thing. We read the Word slowly—in one verse, one creature, one face, one journey, one song—as *one* cosmic story unfolding with grace as our guide.

PART I
GAZE

READING THE WORD
ON THE FACE OF CREATION

*"Gaze . . . look upon and follow the one
who made himself contemptible for your sake."*
—ST. CLARE OF ASSISI

"In the beginning (in the beginning of time to say the least) there were the compasses. Whirling in void their feet traced out beginnings and endings, beginning and end in a single line. Wisdom danced also in circles for these were her kingdom. The sun spun, worlds whirled, the seasons came round, and all things went their rounds; but in the beginning, beginning and end were in one. And in the beginning was love. Love made a sphere, and all things grew within it. The sphere then encompassed beginnings and endings, beginning and end. Love had a compass whose whirling dance traced out a sphere of love in the void; in the center thereof rose a fountain."
—ROBERT LAX[4]

*"God speaks to each of us as he makes us,
then walks with us silently out of the night."*
—RAINER MARIA RILKE

*M*t. Irenaeus, known by many simply as "The Mountain," is our Franciscan community in the hills just east of Olean, New York. The history of our land is layered with mystery, beauty, suffering, and the success of others. We receive this mystery humbly.

When Frederick Douglass, an abolitionist, came through western New York, he preached only a mile from this land. This area was also part of the Underground Railroad and was later owned in the early 1900s by a freed man and a native woman, which was quite controversial at the time. Some of their progeny are buried a hill over. When our chapel was being built, an archaeologist was visiting with his two young daughters when one of the girls noticed something that had been scraped off the topsoil: a grinding stone. Would anyone have noticed if it weren't for a young girl's simple observation? The archaeologist dug it up, examined it, and told us that the site of our chapel was likely a site where native people once gathered seasonally to worship and dance.

When we first arrived at the Mountain, we caught a glimpse of its rich history while exploring the land with students. In a ramshackle barn on our property we were fascinated, captivated, and intrigued by an old wagon wheel we found. The previous owner of the property mentioned that it was probably from the Civil War. This wheel, like most things lying around, had a life before us and had apparently worked hard. We learned that the wheel most likely carried slaves to freedom, and that it was used to transport crops, as the land had

been a grain and potato field around the 1860s. The barn wall showed a similar history of the work of the land.

That evening, we all sat cross-legged on the floor around a wood stove. I can still see our student leader, Peter, searching his mind for an image and reflecting, "Most of us were in the barn today and saw the old wagon wheel." He smiled, sensing that what we saw that afternoon somehow manifested who we are as we circled around him. "The maker of the wagon wheel formed and shaped each spoke carved as its own. *We are the spokes, and together we are the wheel.*"

Those who used the wheel might not be here to tell their story. But the tools they left behind are their objects of hard work and unfold for us a story. Now the wagon wheel was carrying all of *us* to freedom as well. The wheel became a spiritual guide and metaphor—a cosmic piece—as we allowed ourselves to gaze upon it and ruminate on its meaning.

Do you have an image, object, or a symbol in Creation that has become a personal metaphor for you and has helped you discover new meanings?

This uncovering of meaning is at the heart of Lectio. Franciscan Lectio invites us to be open to encounter what is before us, to what might be old but is also full of new meanings.

Our contemplative model of leadership at the Mountain has unfolded with the imagery of this wheel, which carries in it the dimensionality of other wonderful spiritual traditions from the American Southwest to Asia. Whether it be mandalas, mantras, or manners of meaning from functional elements, the wagon wheel seems to hold it all together. We began to imagine the wheel as a map of our cosmos, the intimacy of our circle, the vastness of creation, and our call to enter it. The call beyond our call. The call to others.

What holds the wheel as it spins? What made that old wagon move across the land?

The core of all of this is the axle, this *axis mundi*, an ancient name for the Christ that animates all of us, "the image of the invisible God, the firstborn of all creation. For in [Christ] were created all things in heaven and on earth" (Colossians 1:15–16). The wheel we found was simply leaning against the barn wall, without its axle, without its wagon. This, too, stirred our imaginations.

Have you ever felt as if you did not have a center in your life? This opening—this clear, fresh circular hollow space—calls out for the One who has been, will be, and, for all time, is the axle around which all other things turn and move, by which all things have their meaning. Truly, Christ is the "axle of the cosmos," the axle of the world.

Axles bear the load of the person, the wagon, and move it all across the land. There is a beautiful image here in Acts 17, where Christ is "the one in whom we live and move and have our being." Christ is the axle, the wheel, and the wagon, and he has asked us to be all three as well. There is no spoke without the center and no center without the spokes. We bear our inheritance in him, not only for eternal life, but for living eternally now with others who barely believe they are alive or are on the edge of death.

German-Swiss philosopher Karl Jaspers, one of the early researchers regarding the evolution of human consciousness, worked with the terms "axial" and "pre-axial."[5] Every 600–800 years, it seems humans find themselves in the midst of an axial age—an age that is moving, shifting, almost like a volcano that has its time of an eruption, as the evolution of human consciousness breaches new ground. It is called "axial" because of this movement.[6] The common experience of people in an axial time is that they are feeling the need for new thinking and reflection in order to move on to another way—to make a leap out of a system (or systems) of knowledge, out of a containment of understanding. Many feel axial times come within the human family whenever there is a breakthrough in insight or technology. We are very much living through an axial age right now. The big question is: what is the axle that carries everything forward?

Lectio is a way to sit within the movement, the spinning around the *axis mundi* that is carrying us forward. But there is a *via negativa* aspect to this movement as well. In other words, we can't always see where we're going. It's not that we're not going somewhere. It just doesn't appear as it had been before.

As this book begins, I invite you to let the wagon wheel go with you, as we go with it. Each of us is a spoke, and together we are the wheel. Can you already sense our movement?

WHERE TO BEGIN?

You may have heard someone mention that they fear their lives are "coming to nothing." Most of us have probably felt this existential angst in one way or another. We might be wondering where we came from or what the "why" is of existence.

We are finding a path of meaning—and not only ideas that are meaningful. Some of our meanings strike differences that are not for nothing. They invite us to see the complexities of life, ourselves, and the world around us. And they are not necessarily what we call "logical." They might be self-evident or intuited, but they are here. We are invited to think about them, to reflect deeply, and consider them in our heart.[7]

Franciscan Lectio is not indifferent to the deep questions of love itself, as it looks for meaning. Rather, we celebrate that our differences are expressions of the very "everything" of love's meaning. We do Lectio for love, from love, and in the hope and presence of loving more. Love has a circle, and love circles out or spirals out as an always creative action in the world, which is another way of possibly describing the Christ. *Eros* suddenly appears.

The notion of *haecceitas*—the Franciscan understanding of "this-ness," articulated through our Blessed John Duns Scotus—moves us to see how *unique* creation is. What Scotus means by "thisness" is our lively uniqueness—the way in which God's breath is rising up right now in the persons that you and I are. One of the friars in our community often says that "we are the apple of God's eye, and God cannot take God's eye off of us."

Lectio Divina is a significant and rediscovered practice, for practiced and unpracticed anthropologists! It is for all who wonder where we came from, where we are going, and what we can do about it, and it asks the question "Does it make any difference?" Lectio typically tips us off and lends to us the meaning of great texts of prior peoples who wondered, in their own culture and time, some of the same things we wonder today.

Before books, there were stories and drawings and dances. Art in all its forms helped humans in their earliest discovering. So, what do *we* mean by *books*? We are inviting you to reconfigure and relearn how to read—to perhaps look up from a book and out to the world. The world in which we live, our experiences in the world, creation around us, and the relationships we've been gifted are all "books" on the shelves of our lives. Our lives hold up these books, and these books hold us up as well. We take them down and open them up for one another, don't we? Perhaps in the late hours or over a special lunch or in the car as we drive, a story starts; it unfolds again; it has new color; and meaning is born. This is Lectio. We might think of it as reading an interior map: coming upon ancient directions laid down within us, within creation, and within text, written there by the one who is the Word.

When we start at the very beginning, "the very best place to start," we begin in the hands of an Almighty God who breathes into us through "his" Word: the Christ. The beginning of John's Gospel speaks to our origin: "In the beginning was the Word, and the Word was with God, and the Word was God. He was with God in the beginning. Through him all things were made; without him nothing was made that has been made. In him was life, and that life was the light of all mankind. The light shines in the darkness, and the darkness has not overcome it."

We can sense here the beautiful Hebrew word *ruach*, which is feminine for the creative breath/wind that birthed everything and all of us out of the void. For Christians, this would possibly be a prefiguring of the Holy Spirit. The "Word" that John is pointing us toward envelops us, as many Franciscans have noted, as a cosmic love that was present at the start, and has always been present, even 13.1 billion years before the person of Jesus walked across the planet Earth. As Richard Rohr points out, the Word was the animating force in both incarnations: Creation itself, when God breathed the cosmos into existence, and in the person of Jesus Christ, God Incarnate, who taught us how to live as humans who are one with the Word, animated by the Spirit. Lectio, then, is simply reading the Word. In sacred Scripture. In Creation. In relationships. In the world. In life.

Michael Glazier writes about "the power and dynamism of God's creative function," as revealed in Genesis 1 and Psalm 33.[8] John McKenzie echoes this notion when he writes about "the Word as the creative agent, not common elsewhere in the New Testament"—the very "summit and fullness of the self-revelation of God through his Word (John 18)."[9] This cosmic origin is a reminder to us that, though this book unfolds in quadrants, our movement in Lectio is not only linear, but also spherical. It begins as we do, and in the Word made flesh who dwells among us and—without losing a beat, a step, or a handhold—reaches to the sun, moon, stars, and far beyond.

One of the geniuses of Lectio is its simplicity. We begin a time of Lectio Divina to enter more deeply into the wholeness of holiness in our day, into life with the God by whom in Christ "all things were made." This is not a dizzying circle dance. If we enter with hearts wide open to the Word, it is a spherical adventure that Robert Lax was offering in his poetic story of "The Circus of the Sun."[10]

And in the beginning was love. Love made a sphere: all things grew within it; the sphere then encompassed beginnings and endings, beginning and end. Love had a compass whose whirling dance traced out a sphere of love in the void: in the center thereof rose a fountain.

So, in Lectio, we value all that is "between the covers" of the Bible and between (and under) the covers of our lives. What we uncover as we open to the substance of the story is perhaps the smell and taste of the glory that God has placed in our hands to make available to one another. As Paul wrote in his letter to the Colossians, "Christ is all and in all."[11]

Back in 1960, when I was entering my freshman year at St. Bonaventure University, I had not picked up, let alone held a Bible. I was intimidated by the layers of hierarchy in the church. I didn't know the Word was so accessible! I was hyper respectful of who got to go where, hold what, and be close to sacred things. The Bible, I figured, must be one of those things reserved only for priests. I was not angry, but I was intimidated.

I began to read the Bible for the first time and truly became a student. I wanted to practice what I read. I began to hold the words. I began to have the words hold me. The Word formed and created a world I began to experience, and when I began to experience the world, informed by the Word, I felt a concurrence and a companioning of both the experience and the beauty before me, in the wonder of the world, and the promise spoken of in God's word. We are kin, and in this kindred relationship, we have the first language of the sacred text deep in our beings.

Are you looking at the Bible as a collection of stories, covenants, characters, and words? Or might you also have a sense that there is a profound unity that has come about by the Creator of this communication? This is the One who *is* the covenant we've entered into. Now we are called to be actively involved in that covenant. In Lectio there is a movement from words on a page to the wonderful truth of presence—God's company *to* us and *for* us. Might you take a moment and let that movement happen for you? See if there's a simple shift from many to One, from the multiple to the unitive, from lots of pages to one profound unfolding story. Now we would forever live with the Author of this sacred text and all creation.

As we learn to read again, my guess is that many of us are coming from two spiritual backgrounds, especially if we were raised

Christian. The first is like my own experience: maybe you have felt as if there is distance between yourself and that which is sacred. Catholicism has sometimes felt too impersonal, as the emphasis on practice often leads to simply "going through the motions" without engaging the heart, mind, or senses. I invite you to open the Bible and gaze upon a verse or a story. Savor the Word on the page and let the text break open your world as God is revealed as not only accessible but also intimately involved in your life. The second background might be the opposite: maybe you have felt as if God could *only* be accessed through the Bible or through your mental faculties. Protestantism has sometimes felt too linear or dogmatic, as the emphasis on theology or correctness or even Bible study has formularized spiritual experience and dulled our wonder for God. I invite you to open the Word beyond the page and gaze upon creation, relationships, communication, life, and the world. Treat your life—your meals, your daily commutes, your conversations in the home or boardroom or cubicle—as if you are reading something as sacred as the Bible!

We might begin to ask ourselves the question "What really is the 'first language' of love?" What is the one way in which God is speaking to the many—to all creatures and all creation? We were made for love, by love, and we "do" Lectio to grow in that love that is beyond all words—that "surpasses all understanding" (Philippians 4:7)—that love that we long for and is already ours. All these paradoxes are not resolved, nor do they dissolve completely on their own either, though they are somehow in the God of love who is the One in whom we open the Word, the Christ.

Lectio is part of our walk of freedom, and, as we sit and hear the Word together, we come to read all of life and each other—more fully and more richly—for we are one. Lectio feeds us. So many of us long for this food, and we gather around the table together for bread. Though I write this as a Christian, I think fondly of those who are not: those who have sat beside me and fed me over the years, like the circling within a kiva—a sunken common area for the Pueblo people to gather. What I love about kivas, though we have treated our indigenous people horribly in America, is that everyone is included: all the local people, young and old, assembling around their values. In the cosmology of the native people, their sense was that as they came together, all the cosmos was with them and that they were with the cosmos, which is to say the order and ordering of everything was in their midst. Our ancestors' spiritual imaginations were often much larger than ours.

The story has been told that St. Francis of Assisi once visited a friary at Christmas time, and, in his own exuberance, entered the refectory/dining hall. It was, as friaries were then, quite poor and simple. In that place, on Christmas Day, people were sulking a bit, possibly more conscious of poverty than celebration. Francis took what remained as the only piece of meat in the house, raised it up, and rubbed it on the wall of the dining room saying, "Today it is the celebration of the Incarnation, even the walls should eat meat in celebration."

Francis was a fairly short man but was always larger-than-life. This gesture reaches across generations and helps us feel how something as simple as a word or two from Scripture or a meaningful conversation, rubbed on the walls of our hearts, can bring our home alive. It can bring us out of our sober sense of the day, perhaps out of an idiosyncratic or narcissistic state of mind, and expand our thinking to "hear the Word so that we might live the Word."

With Lectio Divina, as with life itself, this is where we are all "beginning and ending" (T. S. Eliot).[12] It is all about being here to read what is before us. We grow in our attentiveness, quieting our breath and mind. Our senses become even more alert, wakeful. It is interesting that as we quiet our senses, they do not become somnolescent, but they become alert and attentive. We are more and more here, receiving everything—each voice and sound as it exists singularly and less as a crowd of mass noise. We begin to hear in the richest sense. And yes, in Lectio Divina, we begin to hear and read "the voice of God." There might be a lot going on in our lives, and in the world, but there are noises in the other room, or perhaps downstairs, or maybe outside, and we are gathered by the grace of longing and anticipation—that the Word might come to us alive and active in our hearing.[13] Less and less apt to deny others their voice, we begin to hear God's voice in and through "other" voices. What we have called the internal disposition asks for remote preparation. It is time for an understanding of our openings and closings and our beginnings and endings.

READING BEYOND WORDS

In a book about Lectio Divina, it is no secret how important it is to pause and take some time to consider reading again—to realize that core to reading is actually listening. Not so much as a kind of "listening" that analyzes, but more than that: deeper reading that has us feel the sounds and place—the coloration and incarnation while moving through a storyline. As we all know when we are absorbed in a good novel, there is so much more to reading than facts and details. Reading is an experience. It asks us to see, touch, and feel within us. It also prepares us for our life where words do not always lead to solutions or give us processes of analysis that would direct us toward success.

Reading opens up for us the notion of *paradiso*—the garden where we go with our joys and our troubles. Reading with a Franciscan Lectio posture—taking it all in—is a return to the garden, even if it is just a simple paragraph or the simple sway of a tree or stopping at a traffic light in a crowded city. Part of the strain of being human today is that so many things fight for our attention. We have become creatures who conceptualize everything. Ideafication is one of our parlor games, and it has snuck into our spirituality. But in this stance of reading—of openness, of becoming vulnerable to the moment—we are able to receive the world around us. We look up from the page, and with the Word, we have read and received the world. More than our "head," our heart can hold the intimacy of this mystery. St. Bonaventure encourages us that our *"mens"*—our center or core—holds it all, and this frees us to read with more than our minds. As he writes near the end of his prologue to his *Itinerarium Mentis in Deum*:

> *First, therefore, I invite the reader*
> *to the groans of prayer*
> *through Christ crucified,*
> *through whose blood*
> *we are cleansed from the filth of vice—*
> *so that he not believe that reading is sufficient without unction,*
> *speculation without devotion,*
> *investigation without wonder,*
> *observation without joy,*
> *work without piety,*
> *knowledge without love,*
> *understanding without humility.*

You and I might think of this as a "new literacy." It moves from the primary focus on letters and their ability to construct words (which construct sentences, paragraphs, pages, etc.) to gazing upon life and the world. As a hermit, Thomas Merton wrote more about the birds around him than the Scripture he was reading. We realize, as he did, that reading means far more than conceptualizing a book. This new literacy immediately embraces the notion of sacred and divine Lectio, the holy and graced reading of every moment, including what we call the Holy Scriptures. This is a practiced insight as well as a practiced activity. If we begin to have a new literacy about ourselves and read the largesse of the world, then our literacy begins to be multidimensional. As Paul Simon wrote in "The Sound of Silence," we might experience the Word "on subway walls and tenement halls." Reading in this way—as family and members within one story— invites wonder into our lives, and, in this, we might experience something of love and liberation, gratitude and grace, peace and presence.

Have you considered reading beyond words? Pope John XXIII and Pope Paul VI urged the church through Vatican II to "read the signs of the times." Pope Francis lifts this theme up again and continues to exhort us to be not only listeners but *readers* of meaning in the world around us. Can you already sense the play we are having with the words "to read"? We are being invited to expand our sense of things. Pope Francis's encyclicals *Laudato si'* (2015), whose title comes from St. Francis of Assisi's Canticle of the Creatures, and *Fratelli tutti* (2020), which comes from how St. Francis addressed his brothers and sisters, remind us how St. Francis read the Word *in* the world around him. Within them is St. Francis's loving activity of *attendre*—an attention to, or, as you will read later in the words of St.

Clare, a careful kind of "considering." Each and every creature around us—through the Christ, in its own *dispositio,* or disposition—has us stand before a world which is larger than our books.

We, too, in this new literacy, could do the same. Why? Because St. Francis's redeeming message can change our world today—in our relationships with one another and the natural world around us. We are men and women who are to read—to read *before* we hear the Word and *after* we have heard the Word, so that we can read *beyond* hearing the Word *in* a world that needs us to proclaim and live according to the Word. This takes a lifetime, indeed, and a particular type of patience. There is this radical reality that listening and taking time—indeed the "power of slowing"—will open our hearts to see more clearly and to see what is in the world that, at times, is beyond anything we would want to see.

You might be thinking that this is an interesting application of the word "read." This new literacy invites us to consider what it *really* means to "know." The Hebrew sense of "coming to know," is to experience intimately, to enter into love making, as we sometimes call "intercourse." The word we use for knowing is that strong of a word.[14] This kind of knowing, as we can see, does not so much move away from what we call "head knowledge" as to first be grounded in the body, the earth, and human activity. Our culture is very uncomfortable with intimate experience and more interested in gaining head knowledge or "being right." We are to read what is laid before us . . . what stands around us . . . what is within us . . . what the world is made of . . . and what is going on in this moment. This is where the Word is. This is where the Word comes to us.

The bigger task is to "fall in love again," to experience the joy of the journey. I believe that's what it really means to "come to know" as we read. Would you and I, right now, dare to believe in a God who is still falling in love with us? That in this moment God will not take God's eye off of us? That is not a statement of policing our lives or the strenuous activity of making sure we are in line. It is love offered to us here and now. We get to read this love and experience it with all of our being.

Murray Bodo, OFM, opened up this idea to an international audience in a now-classic book for those who wish to follow Francis, *The Journey and the Dream*.[15] Richard Rohr more recently expounds on this in his book, *Eager to Love,* which was inspired by Pope Francis. I dare say that we are made to fall in love with God and everything else around us. This isn't predestination; it's pre-inclination that rises up from the very wonder of Christ's own unfolding and our conjoining with his mother's "yes." St. Francis, a pre-modern man with a postmodern attitude, models this for us. This is the Francis who once climbed up a mountainous hill—discouraged at a time in his youth—and, somewhere along the way, experienced a breakthrough of God's mercy; a felt sense of love and compassion in his very midst. He came down from the hill and walked into a little town, a backwater place where people were depressed economically. Everywhere he went, we're told that he kept saying, "*Bonjourno bonagente*," which means, "Good morning, good people." That's precisely the greeting that converts us. It's less about instruction and more about intimate engagement, its ongoing revelation.

As you begin this journey in Lectio, how can you begin to cross that same bridge—from instruction to encounter? As places and people present themselves, it is as if the Word *invites* us into their company to read them. So, the growing in our literacy, in a cosmic sense of the Word as it is revealed to us, is to read with a depth of listening, with the capacity to be attentive. Reading the times—reading life—is an ancient way of multi-dimensional reading.

The Word leaps off the page, and there is no gluing it down again! The Word, the incarnate expression of God's love and covenant, dances with us and reaches out to us and sits at the table with us and walks down the street with us. This is the capacity and direction of ancient Lectio at a time when many people were illiterate. Yet we have so much to learn from them! They were open to images, visions, and metaphors as they appeared in symbols and signs and eventually on church walls and stained glass windows and icons and art forms. Today we might notice the windows in cathedrals because of their beauty, but centuries ago, when most people were not literate, they were used primarily as catechism, helping people to understand the Bible's stories and the faith and right relationships that rose from them.

We might say that this is where this ancient practice with sacred Scripture relates immediately to living a life of justice and peace. It is not turning to instructions but is *entering into* the one who entered *in* to teach us. A core movement toward integrity is to discover unity that is within the word of God of justice and peace, wholeness and fullness, of life revealed for each and for all. This again is a matter of reading, an ability to see, and, in reading, to wish to be attentive and to apply what we are coming to know through Lectio.

One of the working fictions of our age is that if we work harder and if we bring a complex of resources, we will have won the day! I suspect our eyes are opening right now to the expenditure or misspending of many resources without full communication or reflection. Without this capacity to read—to do adequate Lectio, to seek it out as a sacred experience both for cultural and commercial and particularly for community health settings—we might find ourselves spun out and exhausted. In Lectio, turning ourselves over to the Word, with the Spirit at work within us, with "the Father" (also called "Mother"), we are held in the Godhead. This One enfolds us all. All else falls away in its own simplicity, and we "read" our reliance on receiving the Word. Lectio might not make our problems disappear, but maybe our anxieties are quieted, maybe we loosen our grip on our attachments, maybe we minimize unnecessary suffering. In Lectio, our selfishness or narcissism fades as a certain freedom in connectivity emerges. Our capacity to listen and be present widens, as we make room to help others carry their crosses. We are freed from our fixations and reawakened to the One who fills us up with divine breath. Lectio invites us into slowing, into the empty space where we are attuned to the Word that is rising up.

Could you and I allow *slowing* to hold us and quiet us—to actually move *into* us and our hearts? It is not unusual to feel discomfort or even desperation—to feel the hunger of needing more as we slow. Slowing creates space, and if we don't run from the emptiness, we might feel ourselves feeling drawn closer and closer to the Sacred— that which is unnamable, undefinable, and, in fact, almost empty. It is what receives us and, if we wait long enough, is the very one that holds us.

St. Bonaventure presents the image of a God who is literally "over the top," a God who is "fountain fullness"—an overflowing God, powerful in generosity, a giver of all good gifts. This is our life and baptism, which means "plunge," not "sprinkle." God's fountain, a basin of living water, flows as life, down and out to you and me. All life has come forth from one fountain.

THE SAN DAMIANO CROSS:
The Opening of Lectio for St. Francis and St. Clare

The Cross may not be central to your faith. That's just fine. But it was crucial for St. Francis and St. Clare. The Cross—a sign of the ultimate offering of God in Jesus Christ's dying and rising for us—is a symbol that Christians believe carries a universal proclamation. The Cross is a central message and apparent contradiction in our Christian faith. The Gospels and the Acts of the Apostles unfold this meaning for us. It is in dying that we will live. Walk with me further and consider the Cross as Clare would suggest, not so much as an object of faith but more as an unfolding, involving, and engaging expression of Jesus Christ.

There was an old Cross called the San Damiano Cross that hung in the small wayside chapel of San Damiano down the hillside from Assisi. The Cross—a Syriac painting, possibly a Russian iconic style from three centuries before Francis—is quite striking for a number of reasons. Here before us is Christ crucified, and, truly pivotal to this particular iconic portrayal, Christ is open-eyed, having been put to death on the Cross, but, in this image, he is also buried and now risen from the dead. The Christian mystery is "captured" in this piece of art. Icons move us into the word *logos*—that's why they say you "read" an icon. By fine painting and allusion, we are carried through the primary mysteries of Christ's crucifixion, death, and resurrection.

The Cross for Clare becomes a door and a window, or, as she says, a "mirror." The deep meaning of the Cross—this dying and rising of God in his Son, this saving of us (which is to say the healing of us in body, mind, and spirit and bringing us into the new realm of

God's kingdom)—all unfolds as a contradictory sign. Let's follow the trajectory of Francis and Clare and open ourselves to the possibility of intimate encounter with Life as it unfolds.

Can you recall in your own life a recent moment of quiet? Perhaps something that caught you off guard? Maybe it was an image or a sound or a felt sense of connectedness to a larger world. You might find this deep meaning rises up even now as you reflect. This would be a simple way in which you might visit the experience of one who, like Francis and Clare, sits before the Cross.

I encourage you to trust your own walk. Open yourself up to what seems to speak to you. Whether it's a sound, a sight, a smell, or an image from another religious tradition, let it unfold what it might. Let it speak to *you*—this is the core of Lectio.

With most practices, there is a wonderful sense of a beginning, middle, and end. Lectio is a movement more than it is a practice. Yet as a movement, it has practice about it. Lectio is the ongoing activity that allows us to create a sense of habit with our hearts and minds. Opening sacred Scripture and sitting with it as it stirs our hearts, we deepen our ability to let go. What did it enliven in me? How does that now lend something to this moment in Lectio? Is there a relationship or a convergence of meaning that is happening without my even thinking about it? Am I letting Life speak to me as this living Word is speaking to me now?

Many who take time with Lectio know that it helps to fashion a place not unlike how birds make nests—one that is a place of repose and safety, but also a place where life comes forth and eggs break open! A style of reading or listening invites us to a moment when our hearts might break open and new life comes forward. Lectio might not be a dramatically emotional time; it may be a fairly tranquil one, and the surprise might be a gentle one. Or there might be none of this, just the rising of wonder—a simple gratitude that we have sat awhile with the Word of Life and let life speak to us in all its forms around us and within us.

Since the Cross is truly pivotal—truly *axial* in a cosmic way—we might imagine it standing and spinning while inviting us into stillness. Images can do this! If we truly pause to experience its beauty, *here,* in a particular piece of art, we might encounter what feels like a stoppage of time. Merton speaks of this when he comments on *tempest verge*—a virginal time or point, this inner space of significant solitude and silence from which one begins again. It is from here that Merton and others suggest reality opens up (and out) from there to all of creation.[16] What I find myself calling a "free and open space," invites us to, as Bob Lax would say, "rise and come into the field." This virginal point is not emptiness. It is an anticipatory stance in the dark mystery of abundance, which is always the Word, who is forming the Cosmos.

Before the Cross, you and I enter the mystery of Christ, who overcame death and brings us home to the Father. Christ is the Tree of Life, and each of us is a cosmic flower of the new Tree of Life. Suddenly we might find ourselves gazing upon the Cross like the women who stood beside Jesus at Galilee, the "Marys" who looked up at him. The Cross and the movement of this pole—this post, this beam that is the axle of life and death for Christ, this sacred movement, this violation of God in Christ—has now been transformed into a sacrament upon which Christ hung to make the Father's love for us clear and redemptive in a truly overwhelming way.

Francis found his whole world here—indeed the cosmos in the Christ, and in particular in the Christ on the Cross. Our history tells us that in a deep and almost desperate encounter before the San Damiano Cross, Francis was pleading with the Crucified One, "Lord, what would you have me do?" A voice somehow spoke to him and said, "Francis, do you not see that my house has fallen into ruin? Go therefore and repair the house out of love for me."[17] In our own Lectio practice, we might not hear something so directive yet *in-sight* might rise up nonetheless. And it might be just as experiential and intimate and even mystical. May we begin to open ourselves up to this possibility of encounter? There was an *axis mundi* around which life was moving and spinning in the time of Francis and in ours now as well.

This is a large, sweeping movement of love—*of* the Father *with* the Spirit *for* the Son—that encircles all of us and holds us, enfolds us, along with the sun, moon, and stars. This is the God in whom "we live and move and have our being."[18] And again, there is one axle *to* all that is *in* all of this: the only begotten One.

Like her soul brother and spiritual father, Francis of Assisi, Clare found all that she was looking for before this Cross as well. The Christ of this cross led them to lepers and further into love for all the world. She found her path to God in Jesus Christ and drew other women into her habit of life when they were restricted to a more monastic expression because of their gender. Yet they, too, might have said, "Hold onto your hats, open your hearts, we are on our way!" This is the excitement of Lectio.

In "Circus of the Sun," the beginning (Morning) of Bob Lax's beautiful poem has similar "spinning" imagery, full of incredibly peaceful and playful images.[19] We might begin to hear more about Christ as an axle if we understand Christ as love—the very compass and centering of all things. As St. Irenaeus wrote, "God makes, man is made. As Wise Architect and Sovereign King, God creates from nothing all that is, ordering opposites by his artistry. His plan unites disparate elements from creation to Christ."[20]

At times we have restricted Lectio to sacred text, forgetting that the early "texts" for many people were mosaics, paintings, statuary, and windows. For pre-axial people, it was also lakes, lightning, fire, and cold, as well as the movements of other creatures by way of seasons and sounds. If we step back with Lax's friend Thomas Merton into the church of Saints Cosmas and Damian in Rome, we might enter a cataclysmic experience through the mosaics, not unlike the Lectio that St. Francis and St. Clare were doing with the San Damiano Cross. In Merton's autobiography, *The Seven Storey Mountain*, we read that he was enamored with the pictorials of faith in the dome of the entranceway. It was there that Merton, though not yet "converted," began to encounter this compass—this One who somehow included, held, and circled the world and all of the cosmos. As Merton was "taken in" by the beauty of the art in this church, he wrote that he was thrown off kilter and almost lost his balance, his inner orientation shifting as he entered deeper personal stages of searching for a new *axis mundi*—a new axis at the center of his world and universe. We are beginning to sense the dizzying journey of Christian contemplation in its apparent complexity as it moves to simplicity. Returning to Lax, it is this swirl—this love—that has a compass. A compass only moves if it has an axle, and thus, this large, cosmic movement that we are talking about is very much moving around the axis, the pole of love that is Christ.

Opening up in prayer, meditation, and contemplation, Merton's spiritual search, you might say, began in *conversatio*—honest conversation. In the Church of Saints Cosmas and Damian, he was intimately engaged in how he read the world around him, trying to find the One he was called to, even without a Bible in his hand. These settings for prayer and liturgy came alive for Merton, and something was coming alive in him. I don't think it is a stretch to look at St. Francis's journey as one of visual Lectio alongside this experience from Merton. Though centuries apart, they both lived unsettled lives as young men, to say the least. Both were "taken" by women, but found themselves following "Lady Poverty" and "Lady Wisdom" as friend, companion, and bride. Francis did not have an education as Merton had, yet both studied the world and were keen observers of creation, gazing upon the singular—the individual creature, not a blanket notion of nature. It was not many birds, it was one in particular for Merton and for Francis. Both had great love for and honored Mary, the mother of Christ. Both ached to death over the brokenness of the Church, creation, and the human family.

Eventually both formed much of the inner peace and longing for peace for others, and found God as their core, center, and axis of peace, the very pivot of their world, the center from which they lived a life of conversion and transformation. Both show me something of the human capacity to *watch, wonder, wait,* and *work*—other movements and actions of cosmic Lectio. Lectio invites us to go at our own pace. The power of slowing is watching and wondering and waiting and letting spaciousness open to us without forcing anything to happen.

This event before the San Damiano Cross, when he received the call to rebuild God's home that had fallen into ruin, was a personal, pivotal experience for Francis. Solitude helped Francis's path become more singular and centered and moved him along when he seemed to be making a mistake in understanding God's call—God's inspiration for him. In Francis we find someone who is human and relatable, with his moods and laments that at times overshadowed his song and jubilation. Can you think of other saints whose humanity encourage you to trust *all* of your humanity? As we go about the practice of Lectio, we enter more deeply into our own lives. Receiving the deep sense that God loved him, Francis more and more felt a longing to be generous with himself in the service of God and others. This event before the San Damiano Cross, when he received the call to rebuild God's home that had fallen into ruin, was a personal, pivotal experience for Francis. Christ became more and more his axle, the very core of his being, the one around whom lepers were central to the wheel of love, now giving Francis a vision, with everything moving and having meaning in the Poor Christ.

From there, Francis began doing Lectio (though possibly he wouldn't have called it that) under oak trees and in public places, in the quiet gathering of brothers at night or in chapels, but also in the midst of life's activity when his eyes would fall upon a face or see someone in need, and certainly when he came upon lepers. All of this had him see in order that he could read, listen so that he could be able to hear, and begin to feel life so that he could begin to respond fully to it.

Early Christianity celebrated that "God had become man so that (man) could become God." Francis and Clare sensed this and learned it through their own walk through doing penance and growing in openness, through reading the world around them as well as Scriptures, and especially through the San Damiano Cross. The clear, simple flow of faith given—the coming of the Anointed One—was, and is, an anointing of all of us and all creatures. St. Irenaeus, St.

Bonaventure, Ilia Delio, Richard Rohr, and Murray Bodo, among others, open up for us this flame burning in wonderfully clear language, each a living bush on fire in their own way, inviting us to know a profoundly personal, enfleshed, divine One who came to us.

The simplicity of this—its singularity—is not to be missed. Some authors say the birth of the Franciscan order was a movement that shone like early apostolic times. Both Francis and Clare were in a deep sense of discovery in a time when those "responsible for religion" were caught up in all sorts of political and economic affairs. People from all walks of life were struck by the truth they witnessed to the simple breaking into all our lives by a God of love.

We return to the San Damiano Cross with the blood of Christ still wet on the wood. It portrays a graphic (but not gory) image of one who has been crucified, died, was buried, is risen, and is still bleeding. There is a tranquility about Christ's face, his demeanor, and his body. The iconic form calls us into this tranquility—a deeper sense of serenity and peace through the turmoil. We are drawn in by the pain and suffering of Christ's own death—and through our own—to find our way to paths of peace with Christ.

It is out of time, and thus representing all of time. The sequence of events of Christ certainly are not linear and yet we speak of them that way. The San Damiano Cross helps us to glimpse a nonlinear truth. We might refer to the spherical or the spiraling of God's love up, out, and through the mystery of Christ's birth; his days as a teacher and preacher; his death and resurrection; and here, with him still wide-eyed among us, his calling us forth. The center of the cross, still beating, is the vibrant heart of Christ. Clare, too, turns to the cross, not as a pious image, but as "the way of Christ Jesus." In common parlance, the Cross invites us to "pivot" in our own lives.

Our spiritual masters[21] take us to "school" by placing us before ancient icons, mosaics, and a crucifix, and here again we learn the core "heart dynamic" of Lectio Divina. These pieces of fine art are reflections of a maturing spiritual movement and companion to us on our journey today. This can be both unraveling and revealing! It stirs us to see things as they are. This is exactly the point of Lectio: to see things not as we think of them being, but to venture beyond (and beneath) our seeing and thinking, and to accept that invitation again and again.

In the Franciscan insight found in Francis and Clare, the Christ on the Cross is part of this huge swing or sweep of God's love. John's Gospel, which Francis loved, is often thought of as an "arch"—the servant sweep of the creative power that has redeemed us. It is all here, as it is all in Christ Jesus's passion in/on/with the Crucifix. As we see in Francis's life, his "Lectio moment" before the San Damiano Cross expanded his Lectio practice as his journey unfolded. This is what Lectio does. Little by little, Francis gained the insight that the church he thought he was divinely told to repair was really the home of God, which is the body of Christ, the Corpus Christi, for *we* are God's dwelling now. The San Damiano Cross is the Franciscan catechism and one of our primary teachers of the mystery of our brokenness being beautiful and transformed. The Cosmos is still unfolding and being healed.

THE QUADRANTS OF ST. CLARE

During Clare's lifetime, Agnes of Prague, a woman of noble status, was in the midst of her own search to understand what God would want her to do with her life. She was torn by the expectations of church leaders, her own family, and those whom we'll call "secular authorities." She was attempting to form a community of women in Prague and had gained the counsel of St. Clare of Assisi and her "Poor Ladies" who lived there, a bold and counter-cultural move for someone of her social status.

Clare was notably not a "cleric," as defined by "office" and gender, though she was well educated and probably read and wrote better than Francis. She had actually joined Francis's brotherhood before she was forced outside by church authorities who wanted to "protect" her and other women by a more formal way of life. The fledgling fraternity was big enough for sisters to join, but religious life, as it then was conceived, apparently was not. But Clare was rooted in the freedom and hope of the gospel, and she and the "Poor Clares" ended up becoming more monastics than wanderers.

In Clare's letters to Agnes of Prague, we read that one of her main Lectio practices was being present to the San Damiano Cross. Clare spent most of her days in San Damiano, particularly in a chapel partially restored by Francis and his brothers, which became a monastery for Clare and her sisters. She lived there for forty or more years after Francis, that wandering preacher hermit who, when his own life was coming to an end, came near again to his sister, Clare, and wrote one of his most beautiful pieces, "The Canticle of Creatures," in a little garden by San Damiano.

Clare's series of letters to Agnes of Prague have been studied by persons far more prepared than I for an academic discussion, such as Sr. Margaret Carney and Sr. Joan Mueller. To me, Clare's letters articulate a uniqueness that is truly Franciscan Lectio, what I call a "transportable event." There is, as the brothers had, an itinerancy about it. *It moves.* It moves with us and calls us out to move into the world, having first moved into the mystery of the dying and rising of Christ—this mystery of Christ's own passage into the world. And so we, too, are called to imitate him, follow him, and do as Jesus the Christ did.

In her letters to Agnes, St. Clare draws from her contemplative experiences before the San Damiano Cross, though I am not aware of her ever naming Lectio as a practice, nor a configuration of the movements that serve as a foundation for this book.[22] With the Crucified and risen Lord, she did not use the term "quadrants" or objectify a very personal journey. (You may sense by now that I, too, am trying to make Lectio accessible without objectifying the movements or turning this into a "how to" book.) United with the Christ who had her present to the world, I have chosen (for our own sense of movement) to consider four of the *moments* that might also be considered *movements* in the prayer stance she offers us before the San Damiano Cross.

Clare exhorts Agnes of Prague to enter and remain a free woman "in Christ who has set us free." As we slow, perhaps before a cross or a crucifix in our hand, we might consider our own personal journey and the personal meaning of this Cross. Do we sense a movement in this mystery or are we staying in the same place? Do we know that Christ Jesus went from place to place and finally rose and went home to the Father? Are we involved and would we choose to be in this movement of faith which is lively—indeed a living mystery—painted and formed on the San Damiano Cross, meant to be read and possibly wrestled with, but nonetheless revealing God's wonderful redemption of us all in Jesus Christ?

Both Clare and Francis heard or read from this Cross a sense of being sent forth, a vocational appeal. Clare passes her understanding on to Agnes when she talks about imitating or following—acting in accord—in one heart with the Christ crucified for us. Of course, the Lectio that St. Clare invites Agnes to experience does not have to be practiced in front of the San Damiano Cross. One might prefer it to be before a particular crucifix or the Blessed Sacrament. It can be some other image, mantra, mandala, horizontal line, or vertical line. It is a felt sense of the intervention of worlds that would come to a core place to consider. In Merton's language, this place is virginal, still, open. It asks that our deep hearts will begin to read our imaginations as they are stirred by the fire of God's own love for us, in the faith that ignites when that fire strikes us; and in that reading, in that Lectio experience, we might begin to be followers.

Clare's approach is universal. In a recent retreat we hosted at the Mountain for St. Bonaventure University's pre-med students—in a circle of Hindus, Buddhists, Sikhs, and Christians—students chose our text for prayer and Lectio, the very beautiful passage from St. Clare in her third letter to Agnes:

Place your mind before the mirror of eternity, place your soul in the brightness of his glory, place your heart in the image of the divine essence and transform yourself by contemplation, utterly into the image of his divinity, that you too may feel what his friends feel as they taste the hidden sweetness that God himself has set aside from the beginning for those who love him.

The reading goes on, but can you already feel the upswing, the swirl, the movement around an axle that we as Christians call Christ and others might call light, silence, wholeness, or stillness. All is included here, nothing is dismissed. Clare continues:

Casting aside all things in this false and troubled world that ensnare those who love them blindly, give all of your love to him who gave himself in all for you to love, whose beauty the sun and the moon admire and whose gifts are abundant and precious and grand without end.

All of Clare's letters to Agnes have this swirling yet grounded feel, supporting Agnes both personally and professionally in her day, or, we might say in ours, coaching and mentoring this noblewoman.

Clare, as we will read, in a few short sentences in her second letter to Agnes reflects the core of this Franciscan spirituality. She, with Agnes, faces into pain and death so as to see the rising to new life. Whereas the classical understanding of Lectio has "steps" that arose out of the Desert Fathers and Mothers—*Oratio* (to pray), *Lectio* (to read), *Meditatio* (to meditate), *Contemplatio* (to contemplate), and *Actio* (as Clare would say, to imitate)—the content in Clare's letter to Agnes seems to indicate her own understanding of Lectio with her own Franciscan, experiential spin: *gazing, considering, contemplating,* and *imitating.* You might notice that I've intentionally refrained from even mentioning "steps" for Lectio until now because of our tendency to systematize or linearize spiritual practice in our checklist culture. Lectio, for Clare, is a dance of stillness and commitment, as her first letter to Agnes of Prague invites us to experience. Now let's spend time with her second letter, which provides for us the open-ended structure for Franciscan Lectio. Clare writes:

> Look upon and follow the One who made himself contemptible for your sake. *Gaze upon, Examine, Contemplate* (emphasis mine), most noble queen, desiring to *Follow* your spouse, who is more beautiful than the son of humankind and who, for your salvation, became the vilest of men, despised, struck, and flogged repeatedly over his entire body, dying while suffering the excruciating tortures of the Cross. If you suffer with him, you will reign with him. Grieving with him, you will rejoice with him. Dying with him on the cross of tribulation, you will possess mansions in heaven with him among the splendors of the saints, and your name will be recorded in the book of life.

For Clare, Francis, and their followers, what we call "Lectio" always moves toward *actio*—the loving and healing action, the merciful movement toward justice. This is spherical in nature, out from the Crucified One in Christ, before whom you and I sit. She brings us into this sphere of love, around the axle—the primal tree, the pole of the tent. Clare is exceptional, as many mystics are, in her own imagery and language, but she opens the door for you and me to Franciscan Lectio and points to something significant, something truly mystical.

St. Bonaventure points to us a certain way of prioritizing "coming to know," which involves placing ourselves in a place where we might *learn more than to know*—a phrase that came to me on a sabbatical years ago as a simple liberation. In other words, this kind of knowing causes wonder to rise up from our hearts instead of dualism or certainty from our minds. To learn is to enter activity, even if it is dark or unclear or veiled or obscured. You and I journey in trust before the crucifix, a mirror for our lives. We come with our questions. We can be honest and real.

I have tried to extrapolate from Clare's letters this beautiful quadratic movement she shares with Agnes and explore what this also might mean for us in our own Lectio practice. Clare's own understanding of divine love is a compass with four quadrants.[23]

Gaze (look upon): When Clare asks us to gaze upon the crucified Christ, the one whom she had long sat before, she is inviting us into an experience that will unfold differently for each of us. She is inviting us to gaze upon the Christ who has already risen, who has gone on before us into Galilee . . . the Christ who rose from the tomb and entered the world wholly and fully alive. What emerges in her letters to Agnes is an invitation into the core of a beautiful, terrible mystery that is at the heart of all that is created: freedom in the Cosmic Christ. When she says "gaze upon," I believe she is inviting us to open the focal point of our gaze. Clare was not caught up in her sinfulness while looking at the crucifix. She was rejoining the deep call of the suffering, dying, and resurrection of Christ. (She was doing Lectio with the crucifix.) She was looking at becoming one with the axis of the cosmos, the love-pole of life's compass, and in this experience she was able to be a large enough "tent" for Agnes and others. Our minds (our intellect) are fed by this bread of life. Hungry as we are, it does not bake all alone. Again, we see in St. Clare the heart of Franciscanism: a deep, personal integrated journey *within* and *through* Christ and *out* into the world. This initial longing is part of what "the gaze" is, which is not at all a "dispassionate glance," certainly not a "looking at" something or a scientific examination of it. Rather, it is both heartfelt and the total involvement of our person. Clare's place in the world for forty years was San Damiano. Sometimes before the same crucifix of this image is her place in the cosmos. It reveals to her the cosmic arrangement and organization of life and everything made and unmade. You and I, too, might hear her appeal to place ourselves before the crucifix. How can we take the time to be in simple sitting and place ourselves before the Scriptures—the crucifix? How might we allow ourselves to place ourselves before Life as it reveals itself to us—to *be here*? Being is the primary activity in beginning Lectio—that as our body shows up, the rest of us wants to as well in tranquility and serenity. Clare, we read, is encouraging Agnes to give herself over completely to this type of Lectio; to the One who gave himself completely over to and for us. In other words, in giving ourselves away, we follow the pattern of Christ who gave himself away. We gaze upon this sacred dynamic in the cross and already our sadness begins to turn to joy.

Consider (examine): In gazing upon the mystery, we begin to consider, as Clare says, what this mystery means to us and the impact of its reality. This beautiful sense of examining or considering takes us further into this notion of *Gaze*: engaging all of our senses. In considering, we are examining, wondering, relating to, and being before. As we know, Clare was before the crucifix that Francis was before. This before-ness is a significant part of this whole experience. The San Damiano Cross may have been created by another artist with a different background, but it offers us the story in a large, broad sweep: from the suffering, death, burial, and resurrection of Jesus, who hangs on this cross, with still-open eyes, and is, as one author would say, serenely gazing upon the one who is the viewer. And so, considering and examining help us to extend our gaze, but also to begin to view deeply, or, as the Buddha would say of the meditator, "to look deeply into the moment." This begins to save us from our pre-judgments. Everything becomes new in the moment, precisely because it *is* new. We are allowing ourselves to be open to its newness. Other feelings might rise within us, but this is part of the movement. Christ has overcome death and darkness, and darkness has no sting—hallelujah!

Contemplate (awe before fullness): We then fall deeply into *contemplation* that wells up within us and takes us into the wholeness and fullness of God's abiding presence here. Gerald May's beautiful book *The Wisdom of Wilderness* comes to mind for me now. It is an outstanding literary work that uses simple, chaste phrases of the experience of contemplation while camping in rough terrain as death approaches. May's unique image of God's presence as wisdom is, if I understand him, "the power of slowing," as has been mentioned.[24] In what I think of as a modern classic, with the humor of St. Teresa of Avila, he finds in his own dark journey the light that we only find by our own journeying. Our world can feel that way. Contemplation comes with being where we are and finding that virginal moment—that eternal stillness that is also the place where the fire is sparked and creation begins to rise up and out of the primal Christ. Here is where we, by being comfortable in our gaze, sit and contemplate the One who is the "Alpha and the Omega." This movement ebbs and flows as our breath does, filling our body and emptying our body, filling our soul and letting it become empty again. We reacquaint ourselves with emptiness. Contemplation doesn't "know" time or other means of measurement. This encounter is with the living God, who remains a certain darkness, at the same time a fully present light, a "slowing."

Imitate (follow, *actio,* to act): This is where our faith flows out into the streets and villages, into our homes and workplaces, and into our intentionality to follow Christ. We follow the gospel as we understand it or as it has been brought to us. This is not just following Christ's directives or actions, but *imitating* the Christ in an incarnational sense: the poor Christ . . . the humble Christ . . . the rich Christ . . . the Christ fully alive . . . the Christ entering fully into death . . . the Christ at the table . . . the Christ who heals and blesses . . . the One who rises up in our midst now and who calls us into the world. Light comes to our darkness. Contemplation blossoms. We feel the hunger for love and grace and stoke the desire to imitate Christ in our lives. Clare understood that the whole universe comes forth from the fullness of God's love for us, manifest in Jesus Christ, the crucified one. So there is within it the pain of the unfinished business of our own personal lives while the completeness of God is there. Some theologians have called this "already not yet-ness"—this incredible sense of proleptic eschatology. We are completely and fully reclaimed, empowered, and asked to risk ourselves. Yet it is simple progress—the movement of grace, the opening and unfolding of our senses and our ability to read them—that helps enliven our hearts and minds. The movement in all this is toward action.

All these "movements" are baskets we open. We might also consider some movements that reflect Clare's, like the model we practice at Mt. Irenaeus: *Observe, Judge, Act.* Another is *Remember, Reflect, Respond.* And one very personal to me is *Listen, Trust, Follow.* Use whichever model resonates with you. Though I have extrapolated Clare's quadrants—*Gaze, Consider, Contemplate, Imitate*—maybe there is another word or basket that stirs your imagination. Open it, or, better said, let it open you. Or maybe you'd prefer to use no model at all and treat Lectio as more of a philosophy. The choice is yours. This book is not meant to control your Lectio practice but rather inspire it, just as Clare was equipping Agnes of Prague.

When the Desert Fathers and Mothers opened the Word in the desert, or heard each other speak and proclaim the Word, or mulled over the Word on their own, there was a *kairos*—a breaking in of God's activity that would fill them up and form them as brothers and sisters before monasticism had taken shape. These spiritual seekers had left their homes, careers, workplaces, probably families, most certainly society, the church as it might have been expressed at that time, and possibly their wealth and reputation, not unlike Francis and Clare. This is more than foreshadowing, as Thomas Merton would let us know in his essay on Franciscan Eremitism, referenced later in this book. Women and men for at least two hundred years before Francis had found that their lives needed to change as the world seemed to be coming unhinged. Maybe you feel similarly in your own life or in our own world.

The Desert Mothers and Fathers found "more" in the emptiness of the desert and the silent solitude and simplicity of God's word. So did Francis and Clare in their own ways, in their own axial age. This "movement" was one in human history when leaving meant entering; when departing meant beginning again and finding something new. They discovered a more abundant life, even when the natural asceticism of having nothing to begin with pointed to the fullness and bounty of the living God. To discover a more abundant life through Lectio remains our call today.

Even as we seek a quiet place in our own home or yard or woods or chapel, the world cries out for what we find "in secret." Franciscan Lectio lends us the leisure to gaze upon the center pole of the cosmic tent and sense the "axle of the world."

Christ is the "one tree" in our own forest.

What is central in your own forest at this time?

The whole trajectory of Lectio in this holy manner is offered in Clare's unselfconscious movements of her own prayer before this crucifix. Lectio today, as then, renews us as "living stones" for a new church and world.[25] The crucifix for Clare reflects the whole cosmos. It is the core of our Christology and our *paradiso*—the glorious garden, the simple intimate place of God's presence, the promise of heaven and the heavenly banquet, an image that was important to both Francis and Clare.

It might be helpful to think of Clare's quadrants as movements painted on a bouncy ball. You can bounce it as you walk. You can toss it to someone else. You can stick it in your pocket and travel with it. All four quadrants of Clare are not stationary ones. We need not necessarily be seated to "do the movements." Each quadrant, in its own way, is mobile and invites us to move. In fact, it finally asks us to be totally transformed and move into a transportable way of living, to take the gospel out and also to take nothing else for our journeys to be, as our Franciscan Order has invited us to be, "mendicants of meaning."

Our Lectio is a holy journey to life. The *teleos*, the "last stop," so to speak, is not at all a stop, but an opening, this incredible Alpha and Omega that we are welcomed into through the love of God poured out in Jesus Christ. Reading in this way is like stepping into a stream that is always moving. Can you feel the water? Can you hear the water? Can you taste the water? What is it that you sense? In gazing upon a crucifix or opening a Bible or taking time with something that stirs you deep within, you are participating in Christ's call to his apostles in the garden before his crucifixion—to stay and remain with him, to watch and to pray.

Part of Lectio, like running, is stamina. Do we have the stamina to do the waiting? For our senses and curious minds to open? For the inner parts of ourselves to somewhat work in concert with one another? That beautiful harmony that wants to rise up, the operation, we might say, of interior selves, is part of the joy of Lectio. It begins to take on its own reality, as we are able to sit and listen and be quiet and be still.

Picture the image of an outreaching God creating Adam, as in the painting of the Sistine Chapel. Does our faith still have this kind of wonder? There is a certain partnership already between the Maker and the one who is being formed and called forth. Can we feel the dynamic draw between the finger and the hand and know that within that is the empowerment to be part of the shaping of a "new heaven and new earth"?

Lectio Divina is an immediate, real-world encounter with the One who initiated all from the very beginning and authors all that is becoming. Lectio calls us into the habit and pattern of reading this ongoing story—helping us hear, see, and perceive our place in that story so that we become more than "actors." We are co-creators and makers of that which is in God's heart to shape and form. We have received the call "to be attentive" from those who came before us—to become quiet and move into both an inter-silence and inner silence where we prepare within ourselves "a place where God might dwell," as St. Francis would encourage us.

We live in a time of broken systems and struggling persons. Whole peoples, whole neighborhoods, have risen up in peaceful and sometimes violent reaction to concerns and perceived injustices. Ken Wilber helps us know that our mentality is often tribal: nation against nation, group against group. Long into the history of civilized men and women, people are now daring to tell us we are not civil; that we are not loving; that we are not just.[26] For centuries the wound of racism has cried out for a *metanoia* in our society and with it the need for major societal and economic changes.

Lectio might be speaking to you in a social issue. Might you hear it? That is Lectio: an invitation to *metanoia*, this change of the heart. Lectio is a seedbed for the opportunity to come to wisdom and engagement with others who wonder and are seeking to be engaged with the world. Maybe this is why you wish to open an ancient but sacred text.

What holds us together more than fear? What brought us together more than a common adversary? Many of us find ourselves often in a reactive mode and are not happy about that.

But what does it mean to *progress*, to *proceed*, to *prosper* at this time in human history? This is where and when we create small, safe places to risk considering different ways that are not primarily linear or hierarchical. Where is the power? Who has it? How do we share it to transform our world? The irony is that we have been made whole and holy (and others have been lynched and crucified for saying this). What we need, we have—it is near and around us. Lectio Divina cracks open all the treasures that are truly ours. The power of the Creator creating, the potter forming, the bush burning, is forever present in our reading.

Moving through our division, the subject, object, and separation of life paradoxically *help* us when we return to the consideration of Lectio. We have a covenantal text so that we would know that we are totally engaged by—and with—our Divine One along with others who have come forth from that divinity. This is partly an imaginal journey of waking us up from, as Thomas Merton would say, "our life of 'separateness, of spurious self-isolation.'"

Lectio helps us have a felt sense for the world we are in, possibly in the moments we consider to be "ordinary." Perhaps you thought you were taking out the garbage, or letting the dog out, or retrieving something from your car, but then you looked up, and the roof blew off your soul. And for a moment, you could see more of the cosmos than you ever thought. As much as we value our thinking and our ideas, we must continually find reverence.

In his beautiful essay "Learning to Live," Thomas Merton talks about meeting with the prolific Buddhist writer D. T. Suzuki. Whereas Merton, quite monk-like, took time with his tea, Suzuki drained it as if he were throwing back a shot of whiskey. Merton writes, "It was at once as if nothing at all had happened and as if the roof had flown off the building. . . . And whatever you do, every act, however small, can teach you everything—provided you see who it is that is acting."

Lectio, in the Franciscan manner, began with a little Italian man, Francis of Assisi, who called himself an "*idiota*," not having a formal education. Yet he went on to dance and delight and suffer through the very Word of God in creation in and around him. Reading, then, was more about the ability to perceive. This is the activity of Franciscan Lectio; *recogito*, "to know again." Its very first movement—its nascent moment—might be as simple as a person taking out the garbage and being swept into the cosmos.[27] This movement is the grace-filled light in darkness, as we begin to read again in the manner of Francis. Over time, theology and spiritual disciplines often become overly systematized and formulated. The mystics come along and break things open for us (and we would barely believe there is a mystic in us beside the garbage can), inviting us back into divine intimacy—the core aspect of authentic spiritual experience.

As with Merton when he was taken in by the different mosaics, truly reading is like falling in love (*amóre*) with art. It has a way of getting inside you. So, in a sense, there is a kind of "social interaction"—this primal engagement of God with all creation.

Similarly, the sacred Scriptures are woven together, just as a sacred basket would bear its contents. Some of the contents within the basket are almost beyond seeing or perceiving. We are invited nonetheless to open the sacred basket each new day and receive. It might contain what we need to bring from the marketplace to our home, and from our home to the marketplace. Woven of fibers and fabrics, put together from reeds and thistles, these baskets of meaning have made their way to many places. And now the basket makes its way into our hands—for us to open and see what is inside, to experience its spaciousness, even if at first it seems to not be carrying anything. Our Lectio experience itself becomes something for this basket. To experience what is inside is to say we *read* what is inside.

To begin to read again, that is the starting place. It is not a terminus for someone who is already seasoned. Maybe we need to take stock of who we are and our wonderful complications but then open ourselves up again. Before there were written words as we now know them, people were making markings in sand, on cave walls, on large, exposed boulders, and on tree trunks; elements were rearranged, whether rocks or vegetation, to express something. Some of this has remained in what we call early architecture and sacred places such as Stonehenge. To begin to understand this pre-written word mindset, try gazing upon a picture and give it enough time to speak a story to you. Before humans had writing, they were still reading. Before there was writing, still there was Lectio Divina. And before we knew written words as children, we were still reading as well—observing the things around us and the faces of those who cared for us. Hopefully, if we were lucky, we were able to read something of tenderness and safety in our homes. Throughout our lives, no matter our age, we "read" beyond our literacy. We are drawn into the contents of what is revealed far more than our skillfulness to grasp it.

A deep sense of story arose within the markings our ancestors carved in wood or drew with charcoal in semi-darkness on cave walls. These words and markings, even as they fall upon a piece of paper today, invite us to *experience* a deep sense of story. In our lives, "markings" transform and evolve, offering us meaning through all this opening and unfolding. New life comes to each of us as we begin to learn to read, having already naturally learned to read by interpreting faces and voices. Meaning pours out of the pages of books, billboards and advertisements, cell phone and computer screens, as well as nature and relationships.

In Francis's time people thought of the world as more flat than spherical. They believed the world beyond them to be magical, while certainly dark beyond its boundaries. Francis's journey brought him to a God who was not only benign or beneficent but was also overflowing in love and goodness toward each creature, as each creature overflowed with love and goodness toward him. He began to live a life with "no fear" and made passage on roads and highways, over hills and vales, with less trepidation about what was "out there" or beyond his understanding of "here." It allowed him to be present to what was immediate to him on the road and on the pathway. Thus, Francis would pick up a twig or a branch and break into song. He would see a worm on the road, retrieve it, and place it safely on the side of the road.

Perhaps his immediacy to creation came from a soul that was quieted from the fear of its need to protect itself. This itself may go back to his sense of cosmology—the way in which he saw the earth within the breadth of all creation, an entire cosmos though not immediately known or understood, yet still safe and secure in God's hands. He did not see the unknown as threatening. In many ways Francis's naïveté (possibly his own second naïveté) gives us hope for ours—that we can encounter the bright light of God in reading the reality of God in Word and in Creation, and be free of the fear of darkness and be overwhelmed with the wonder of the light of Christ in and through everything and everyone.

Several years ago while I was on sabbatical, someone recommended a book by David Abram called *The Spell of the Sensuous*. Abram had taken time in the beginning of his book to write about where speech comes from, taking readers into the rich world of the sensual—the sensuality of sight and feeling and voice. Humans were not at the epicenter of this paradigm. *All* creatures were finding their way across the earth, even as our planet's face was changing through not only different seasons but also epics and eras. The role of simple sounds and images animates the human adventure of coming to know, coming to question, coming to believe, and making ways of communicating all of these. Meaning-making, as we see, is not a quick practice or event.

It is the time of our second naïveté, after we've passed through a certain darkness and skepticism, that we open again to seeing the simple as fresh as it is revelatory. You and I are on our way. When I was cooking the other day I thought of onion paper—how it is so thin, translucent, and almost transparent. This reminded me of how something organic can allow us to see through, see into, and see beyond. This is the sort of seeing that is also knowing, that Francis celebrates for us in the immediacy and continuity of his senses, particularly when they are directed toward the One, the True, and the Beautiful. This is also the journey of St. Bonaventure while he was on Mt. La Verna. As a great intellect, Bonaventure dives into the created order and takes us with him, later using the metaphor of the "Tree of Life," another Christic icon.[28] Bonaventure's own senses came alive, providing the healing he needed, which he says came from a peace that surpasses all understanding. Like Francis, but a completely different man, a university professor, he tells us our senses are sometimes our best teachers. Francis and Bonaventure were both looking and longing for Christ in all creation. Their posture toward the created order demonstrated that what is here can open the "eyes of our heart."[29] God breathes through everything with goodness and fullness. We find reading to be a sacred activity and an essential one in surviving and being alive. Each moment, each movement, each creature, somehow bears the one who is holy, and offers us a sense of direction—deeper into beauty, into true knowing—if we are able to read it.

Beginning to read again, we read each other's movements and the reality of each other's faces, which are also so sacred, as indeed are our tears. As we build our lives upon sacred reading, we go deeper, we grow older, we develop a greater need of charity and of just living. It is holy to search and find and read all that God shows us of God's self. Indeed, it is a serious activity of wonderful exploration, not only something we do in the place of playing cards. Reading, then, is a holy and essential activity leading us to an active life of holiness and ways of justice and the activities of wisdom. We can be comforted that the cosmos is perpetually coming forth from the heart and hand of God in Christ the Son, the Word of God. We read this movement and find it both on the pages of sacred texts and in the manifestations of life and darkness around us.

Literacy, in the broader sense of what it means to be able to read, takes on new meaning. It does not allow me to be a dilettante: a self-pleased pursuer of new facts and ideas. It is larger than letters. Though we sometimes use words to debate and dominate, we forget that letters and words are larger than we are. No one, with their human mind, has understood every word in every language. Yes, we see words in small businesses and on the walls of warehouses, but the meaning behind the arrangement of letters is expansive. Blank spaces on the outside of buildings are now being utilized in cities and towns for wonderful murals, where letters and words are often painted, reaching far beyond the words themselves, as art often does, and extending the message out to the city and back down into the immediacy of our heart to spring us into a conversation with the world around us.[30]

Our capacity to see and read beyond the words, between the letters—to "read between the lines," we might say (which is that great reference when someone says they're beginning to understand)— breaks open what it means to read. *Through* whom and *in* whom all of this is open to us, it is alive *for* us. As Christians we think of it more and more as the place of profound activity and connectivity. This is where we are one, becoming one, and from there we find the energy and generativity to enter into the fullness of the world. It is how we see and how we read what we're seeing.

How we see (and how we are seen) when we are growing up still impacts us today. People perhaps read us a certain way in our formative years; we caught their message, and sometimes we are still unraveling that message.[31] Lectio, especially as a communal prayer practice, acts as a balm in the sense that it cuts open our unhealthy thought patterns, idols, and attachments. This makes the disruption a healing agent—healing our inner eyes and our inner conversations with ourselves. We gain a vision and a new capacity to read. It becomes truly cosmic because it becomes that intimate. They are both the same, though we name them differently, because that is the wonderful activity of language—to talk to both sides of the moon at the very same time, the dark and the light, and to not disvalue either. They make up one moon!

As was common in society at that time, Francis at first found leprosy repulsive or "nauseating" and "bitter." But what was bitter to him became sweet. Francis gravitated toward the lepers at a transformational time in his own life, setting the trajectory for his ministry. He was stirred to embrace a leper, then kiss one, and, eventually, he would learn to share a meal from the same plate as one. This leper—this *person*—revealed Christ to Francis, as he shared with other friars in his "Last Testament." In the person of the leper, Francis saw and embraced the axle of the cosmos, the center of the universe, and the core of God's love.

Slowly, ever so slowly, we see beauty and goodness. How many of us have been inspired by someone who suffered well or walked courageously through tragedy? Of course we would never wish that on them, but we come to a place of gratitude that our hearts were given the opportunity to *read* an experience that we will integrate into our lives. This is Lectio Divina in the real world that is not just passing by. We are walking through the world with others.

Maybe we've heard it said, "Oh, I can see new life in your eyes!" This mystical movement—this somewhat visual shift—informs how we act. We read each other and the world around us as new. There's a bit of a resurgence of phenomenology in what I'm saying here.[32] A phenomenonologist looks at what is happening—the present experience. When we say, "That is phenomenal," what we mean is that it is dynamically and actively real in our midst. We are all phenomenologists to some degree because we see truth in people's actions. There's an immediacy to phenomenology. Franciscans are hopeful phenomenologists—that God is active, alive, and immediate to us.

People sometimes think that Francis was a pantheist, but he might be better described as a pan-en-theist. Francis saw God in all that God had made, which, as we understand, is all that is. Francis's phenomenology was on full display as he looked for the significance of life in God's activity, the Word in the world. That's why Franciscans are evangelists, called always to bear Good News. God, not ever being passive, wants to rise in these moments, and thus they are mystical.

Franciscan Lectio is about being blessed to be *in* one present phenomenon—to be able to read the world in and through the One who is the Living Word. It is good to pause with this one line and let it reverberate through our whole selves. We become the bell that wants to ring in a world that clambers. We become the voice that might rise up in humble ways to call for peace when words seem no longer to matter.

BEING COSMIC

Being cosmic—what might that mean? Different teachers and traditions offer us steps into what Ken Wilbur calls "kosmic consciousness." Christians consider this primarily in the dawn of Christ's resurrection in each of us and our coming to a whole new way of seeing. We awaken. We arise and come into the field. We come to a fuller consciousness. We commit to "be here now." The radical freedom that is promised in Christ is the fuller notion of salvation, not only from sin. Joy in this consciousness, you can almost feel, moves us out of what we call "self-consciousness" into a curiosity and desire to be engaged in the creative order near us. We begin to enter more trustfully into the whole cosmos—that we might be cosmic in our life.

To enter into our place in the cosmos is to awaken to our interconnectedness with all other creatures—to become aware of all that we are listening and attending to, all that we are *reading*. In this consciousness, we become liberated from our isolation and feelings of separateness that are defeating us. The core of Lectio as practice is our interconnectedness. We are one family with all that has come forth in Christ from the Creator, as St. Francis would say. In many traditions, coming to this is thought of as an awakening, which is also a lovely way to think of Lectio.

In common parlance, "mysterious" can mean "unknowable." Our mysterious God is here to be known differently from what we often mean by "to know," thus this book. As we invite you into our text, we actually are inviting you into knowing the "Great Mystery." Being cosmic, it is at once intimate, close, and able to be "known." It is experiential, emerging from sea to shining sea, across and around, throughout all of creation. In one sense, it's beyond our imaginations. In another sense it invites us to explore and discover and then imagine what it is we are coming upon. We are entering into relationships that are both vibrant and vital. They are real and rich. They authenticate the fact that we are alive on Mother Earth, with many others. At times it has no name. We have no words for this relational mystery.

In Lectio we hear the sounds and voices rising from the cosmos. Some sounds echo from the past, long ago. Some have left vestiges: fossils in places, lovely pieces of skin or flesh, leaves or bark, or whole animals for us to gaze upon and realize they walked upon the earth right where we do today, but many millennia before. We are on what we call "the earth"—this shifting, moving, shaking rock and water that seems so stable in our own universe, which is part of this incredible expanse that we call the cosmos. We gave the cosmos a name, perhaps, because we feel best when we have one name that somehow holds everything in it. But there is no holding all of this. The wonderful thing, as St. Paul says to Timothy, is that the Word of the Lord cannot be chained.[33]

This new literacy is not to diminish our modern understanding of reading. We can hear the power of reading in our vernacular.

"Oh, I can read your face."

"Oh, I saw it in the stars."

"Oh, could you spell that out for me?"

These mean that signature moments we read and see give us a felt sense of direction, purpose, or hope. Whether a situation sounds or feels superstitious, it rarely matters—still people tend to ground themselves in what they read intuitively. We are *already* reading beyond words!

When we, as pre-axial human beings, began to use water and fire (what we now call the elements), before long we began to commodify them. In commodification, we perhaps lost touch with how magical and beautiful it was to our ancestors; yet we also moved into ways of gathering and hunting and bringing about a life that is what we call "human." But all this took a lot of reading, preceded by listening—to the birds and the trees, to the air and to the large stones falling off cliffs, to a river changing its course in the middle of a storm, and to so many other sounds like a breeze combing the grass. These are all sounds that no one can imitate, yet we know them when we hear them—signature languages of the earth for us to read or listen to.[34] How are you tempted to overly commodify different aspects of your life? Could these be the areas where you might learn to read again?

In *listening* we begin to learn how to read. One can only begin to imagine what the voices might be on Mars or any of the other planets, but they are as real as those on Earth, perhaps even older than our planet. In our exploration of the cosmos, this conjoining effort with other peoples is, in a sense, to hear the first sounds of creation—to hear them as they are anew, though the sounds have always been there.

I would call all of this oral Lectio. In listening and hearing these sounds—and possibly the patterns in them—like the birds up in the tree or the wind as it tumbles over a particular hill, you and I begin to read what those sounds mean, what the pattern or habit might be of the earth, of the atmosphere, and beyond. As the hymn goes, "Open your ears, oh, faithful people, open your ears and hear good news."

Are we opening our hearts to each other? And enough to open each other's minds? Most of the time in our world, knowledge and ideas pull the train of experience (whether it be religion, education, or politics), but Franciscan Lectio is more about the heart—how it holds and encounters the cosmos. Do we admire the opening to beauty as a freshly opened blossom, but hold back from heartfelt listening and communicating? It is amazing to consider the implications of listening and choosing to hear the Word in the one chamber where my heart is not divided, then allowing the truth that is heard to permeate the divided chambers. Not only will Lectio, regularly practiced with other sacraments, offer our faith a fresh beginning, but it will also truly introduce us to "living waters." We are traveling in the world, and the world is ringing like a huge bell everywhere—a bell with many voices as the Word of life itself. Compassion cannot be spelled without "compass."

I delight in a certain irony that the Word of God—God's active conversation with us, *conversatio divina*—abounds in silence. The meaning of a few words might become rich but slowly, and often surely, silence emerges as the only way of sitting with the truth of the Word. Then, of course, this is why silence is our path to listening, and, most of all, our way in a conversation.

In my childhood, I learned something about God's Word while in the woods. We would find our way to Genesee River Gorge by listening to Brown Falls. In life there are courses and cascades. They each have their own voice and are speaking with others, part of a chorus that rises up. This is not a static location but is a lively presence that adds to the life of that setting. And so, in the Word of God, there is a new voice joining other voices, singing beside the trees and beyond.

There are many simple places and times where we can hear and believe that the Word of God is "drop down dew, like heaven from above." The Word lands upon us, comes into us, and insinuates itself to us. It is absorbed into our very skin, soul, and body, so that we can listen with more organs—all of them, rather than only our ears. It is important for us to remember, though, that the Word is a great gift and never an intruder. Christ has poured himself out, coming as gift for all of us, but we have received the freedom to open ourselves to the Word of God in Jesus Christ. Our bodies then are lively in their activity and not only passive. Another simple way of saying this is that it truly is an adult activity! It is up to us to listen, to communicate, to be prepared to hear the Word of God. We do this not out of some threat or danger from an almighty being but because of the love and promise of the One whose love is poured out in the Word. The creative power of the Word does not seek to control us but rather bring us further and further into the fullness of who we are. We make our way for hearing by making space for silence and trusting silence.

Lectio allows us to sit (and perhaps swim) in these Living Waters. It is not only poetic when we say that Lectio is a simple, sacred way of breaking open the Word of God as our spiritual food and nourishment. I would say to be born, to begin Lectio, we must first be opened to the Christ and acknowledge that the core of the cosmos and the deepest place within our hearts are already speaking to us. The Father and the Spirit are breaking through and settling in and abiding with Christ, who is the fire of our hearts, in the very wind that moves through us and brings us life. To truly grow up—to foster relationships or families—is to be attentive to all this.

This beautiful sense of abiding is very rich. In this listening, there in the depths of silence, we are moved out of a comfortable modality, meaning that we are not together only to talk or only to share ideas or only to speak about the wisdom we have for the sacred literature or the knowledge we have from the sacred text. Rather, we have gathered, each of us in humble awe *of* each other and of the "thinness" of the moment, around one of God's very real and earliest tabernacles. We sit within the tent that goes with us. We are gathered in the place in which our covenant with God continues to be named, expressed, noted historically in metaphor and in myth; and where we hear the fullness of Christ's life being table, mystery, and ministry.

In Lectio, the notion of time—all the deadlines, demands, and commitments that come with it—fade. We become grounded in this moment. We gather up, in a place *in* time, sinking so deep into the present that it feels as if there is no such thing as time. We open our hearts. This is where the quiet comes in, allowing us to settle. We allow it to find us. We wait. In a sense, we die; we pass over into a restfulness that would open us up to a new springtime in our hearts. This sort of listening takes us to deep places. This vulnerable silence invites us to feel a certain kind of helplessness, a humility, something Thomas Merton called "a little point of nothingness and of absolute poverty, the pure glory of God in us."[35] Though we often spend the duration of our days "calling the shots," thinking that we are in control, Lectio is not a task to complete—it asks us to be open to the One who has opened us and is open within us, who dwells within the temples that we are.[36]

Christ, the Word, is the bread and cup, and now we sit at the table of discipleship. We learn in him the mystery of ministry, and he is our food to serve his body, which, as we are reflecting here, is the whole cosmos, one page at a time. It welcomes Lady Poverty and her sister, Simplicity, to the table. A counter sign to the reality of our time is Francis's love of Lady Poverty. In this union came forth the fruit of a family of sisters and brothers who are called to a simple way of living with, and among, the rich and poor alike.

Lectio, in all its fullness, is a practice that calls for very little: the Word, our wonder, a wounded heart, and the willingness to wander as one in the obedience of Christ. It has its own poverty. It is the Word enfleshed. We are to be transformed as "hearers" and "doers" of the Word.

ON SEEING KEUKA LAKE

Between my junior and senior year in college, when I was still floating in the pool of not knowing, uncertain about what I might do after I graduated, but quite certain that I wasn't going to complete a degree in biology that would prepare me for medical school, I was thinking of the friars. I was in a significant relationship and did not know how to step aside from it easily (though she and I talked about my ruminations of becoming a friar); my head was muddled. I had been thinking of the friars, but if you remember, I was a "public"—a public school student—and had an unspoken identity, a social reality that I was not part of the Catholic community.

I remember it being a beautiful summer day, and our family was completing a weekend at Keuka Lake, a real haven for us. My father asked me to help him collect the garbage from around the place. We would then haul it up the hill to the dump. Yes, it was a dump back then, and there was unfortunately no sense of recycling going on.

"Bill, would you help me out? I would like to get this stuff together and load it up and have the house clear of the smell of these corncobs!"

Getting into the car with him after we packed the trash in the back, I was still bothered by having to make this trip, when I had all these important things about my future to consider. We drove down the lake and took a right, which took us up over a spectacular hillside covered with vineyards and farms. We took another right, which brought us quickly into the dump. As we were opening our doors, my dad, from the passenger side, stood up, put his hands on the top of the car, and looked out over the car and smiled at me. As I looked at him, he called me by name and said, "Bill, look! *Look* how beautiful!"

I looked back at him and thought: *Has he lost his mind?* Here we stood in that stinking dump, and everything we brought had its own stench. I wanted to get out of there—*what could be beautiful about this?* His voice broke in, "Bill, just look! Look around you, look out over there!" as he lifted his hand and pointed behind me. As I turned around, I realized that, yes, there was a dump on the top of the hill above the lake. But from the dump, we had the most perfect view of Keuka Lake. I would say "beautiful beyond expression," except that my dad's face expressed it so well. He woke my heart up to a reality that was beyond the way I was reading anything that day.

This story is a reminder of voices that were speaking to us before we found our way of listening to them. But they are still there, often in our body memory and memory of other stories. Through story, we begin to hear those past voices and see those places. It's not what we would call "sentiment" or "nostalgia," but it is what Bonaventure would call "wonder." When we say to one another, "Oh, that's what you meant," we are hearing each other again but in a new way. That's what we're doing with God as we gain a graced perspective in Lectio. It's like a sacred retrospective, listening and looking again. The monks would call it "mulling over" as if we were chewing our cud like a cow. In this chewing perhaps we taste how someone in our life helped us awaken from our preoccupation and to "taste and see" the goodness of God. How are you tasting what is beautiful right before you and around you?

That is one of the challenges of Lectio and of reading beyond words. Words will barely jar a heart that is stuck somewhere in its own darkness. It is worth pausing here and considering a story in our lives where "that which was bitter became sweet," as St. Francis said of a leper he encountered on the road. What might we see, read, or realize that turns our hearts and minds around?

MAY THEY BE ONE: THE INCARNATION

When productivity edges out poetry as purposeful, we have lost something as humans. Words might be understood only as "meaningful" if they convey "facts." Franciscan Lectio takes us deeper. It resurrects poetry and indeed is resurrected by it. It welcomes it and engages it. With this in mind, consider Jesus's words from John 17: "*That they may be one, Father, as you and I are one.*"

The Incarnation is one of the oldest ways of "looking at" doing Lectio. I invite you here to look at the Incarnation with the eye of your heart, not just your analytical mind; with an experiential openness, not just theology and theory. In gazing upon this beautiful mystery, in reading it as poetry, we become awestruck that God became human and that we humans share in God's divinity, which was an early Christian teaching. We are in the threshold and in the room of the Word, which is lively, holy, and "effective." Purposefulness has had its own popular day, but eternal value seems to be returning to us—what the Word truly is and the Word's deeper purpose, which is union and communion with the One who lives and breathes and makes all things new again.

Now, and with a renewed sense of cosmic Lectio, everything is powerful, rising from its own fountain given by its Creator, a "fountain fullness," as is Bonaventure's image of God. We are creatures bearing light and flowing with love, indeed blessed in sacred darkness of unknowing at times. Now words leave us, or, rather, send us forth. The radical-rooted richness of our experience invites wonder and creates actions in our lives that speak for themselves to us for God! As Jesus said in Matthew 11:15, "Whoever has ears ought to hear." This union/communion is one of the key tenets of the Christian religion (as is said in the book of Acts, "See how they love one another!").[37]

It is "the Word" proclaimed in John 1 and 1 John 1 that has made us one and glories in us. It has fashioned us as a gift to one another and returned us to the Father. Fear tries to tear us apart so that we "believe" more in our apart-ness than we might in our *at-one-ment*. Richard Rohr, in so many wonderful places, comments on this as one of his early and primary themes. Being loved can feel almost unbearable.[38]

We reach back to the Acts of the Apostles, the Little Flowers of St. Francis of Assisi, and other collections of stories—of wandering minstrels and preachers and communities—being formed around the liveliness of the Word and Spirit. In his short article about Franciscan Eremitism, Thomas Merton notes that St. Francis and his movement had predecessors—men and women, penitents and pilgrims, who journeyed through Europe and other places and found themselves seeking the woods and other sites for solitude. They congregated for the Word and probably also for safety. This phenomenon has happened a number of times, and the members of each movement are often drawn into already-established monastic communities. The Franciscan movement is atypical for many reasons but partly because of its strong ability to sustain its charism, its inner dynamic, whose lifetime champion was St. Clare.

Humble and numerous, these human stories awaken in us a sense of seeing. They invite us to "see" how they love one another! We are frail and fail, but we are not failures. This unity can never be dissolved, though it is challenged and at times forgotten as the world confuses us. But God's primary manifestation is in our midst, and we find it again and again in the simple truth of Christ Jesus being one with the Father and the Spirit. This Triune experience is part of what blossoms as we listen to the Word, as we gather in Lectio Divina. We are drawn into this listening in the friendship of this God, who is always listening.

Lectio helps us to practice our coming into unity with our diversity, complexity, feeling, and thinking, helping us to see things differently and listen with a different tone to our ear. There is a blessed ache, a longing that seeks fulfillment in the God who is one. And we can hear that ache in Christ's own words, as Jesus says, "That they may be one, Father, as you and I are one." This rings out again and again, and with grace we are moved by its appeal.

In Christ "we are God's children now."[39] In other words, the theological or spiritual playground of what we are about is quite large and extensive, brought back to the simplest of sandboxes, or the arrival at, not a teeter-totter, but a swing that carries us up into the blue and brings us back down to earth again, each of which are experiences of the Cosmic Christ and the journey within.

The excitement here is because deep within we are artists. Yet most of us have not had our chance yet in life to become what we call "creative." We miss the fact that there is a giftedness about ourselves where our own artistry shines. A beautiful, old definition of art comes from Thomas Aquinas's notion of what is translated as "the right way of making something." This suggests that anything made wants to be beautiful and come to fullness or completion—the economy of form. St. Thomas Aquinas points us toward the simplicity that there is nothing extraneous about true art. Art has an authenticity and simplicity of material and purpose. It accomplishes what it began, which, in itself, is the definition of beauty. It shines before us as fullness and completeness, which is what creation is, as well as God's activity in it. God is our Artist, our Weaver, our Potter. This brings us back to the wheel, which influenced weaving and pottering significantly. The spinning wheel. The potter's wheel.

This is why, in our Franciscan school, creatures are seen as vestiges of God—a place, a sign, a thumb-mark, or fingerprint of the Almighty One who "bends low," as St. Irenaeus lets us know when he calls God a *sapiens architectus,* a wise architect. This is a God who still holds our clay so that it might remain moist, as we feel the hands and fingers of the artist. As St. Irenaeus wrote, "It is not you who shapes God, it is God who shapes you. If, then, you are the work of God, await at the hand of the artist who does all things in due season. Offer him your heart, soft and tractable, to keep the form in which the artist has shaped you. Let your clay be moist lest you grow hard and lose the imprint of God's fingers."

The Incarnation suggests to us that we are swimming in the beautiful, and we respond by seeking to see beauty in every thing. St. Irenaeus speaks of this as the "recapitulation" of all things in

Christ, and here we begin to celebrate the iconic Alpha and Omega. St. Bonaventure and particularly John Duns Scotus also talk about everything coming together in Christ. All that has begun in God in Christ comes to completion again. *All in all.*

As St. Bonaventure encourages, justice is returning something or someone to its original beauty. The Incarnation is happening *now*—it is ongoing and real, and God has brought us into this creative mystery in some real way. All things are being created in and through Christ.[40]

The cornerstone that we are told was "rejected" when Jesus stepped onto the scene remains our great reminder today. As we hear and believe, more and more, that "Black lives matter," one of the great and everlasting messages that arises for me in my walk with our African American sisters and brothers has been this deep awareness of the value and beauty of ourselves being here. The painful irony is that I learned this truth from people who have been rejected *for* being here and placed in subservient places. As Christians, we have a cosmology that has us "read" all that is with its beginning and end in the Christ who is God made flesh. Or, said simply, life asks us to return to our lives; it asks us to risk looking at our own flesh for the monstrance of God's marvelous presence.

There is no duality in God becoming human. God became one of us. Our brother, Jesus, walked this earth; he was somewhat dark-skinned, not tall, not immediately recognizable, certainly not a "White person;" yet we are inclined to see everything through our own eyes of identity. Lectio helps us "look out" to find a way of not dismissing anybody's self-identity but find a new way to common and deep inclusion of rich fullness of identities.

Said more simply, matter *does* matter to God. As I first heard from Br. Bill Short, OFM, God is the Former, Shaper, Artisan, Potter, Creator of all matter. So, God does not overlook anything. Rather, God looks *with* and *into*. God walks with, and converses with all. Every creature remains, first and finally, as an act of their living Creator's love. God leaves no one and nothing alone. "All of us are the glory of God when we are fully alive," as St. Irenaeus tells us.

We are still "damp clay," and we are living in the Divine Artist's hands. Lectio has us look up and out of books and at times to all that is incarnate—the substance of the world around us—and know that this is God's world. Christ is the Word in and through all of this in and around us—the incarnate expression of the Father's love for us.

COMING TO KNOW

Our Franciscan tradition helps us open our eyes to the undervalued wholeness of being a human person and the wholeness of all creation. There seems to be a rediscovery of both scholarly and popular ways to come to know. Much of what we're doing here in this book is longing to know: awakening to a common path, and on that path, discovering new "tools" in coming to know and recover old pedagogies.[41] Education is multidimensional. This is holistic learning, domestic learning.

Our minds are overtrained to do the knowing for us. In our Western culture we are sometimes obsessed with "figuring it all out." When it comes to religion, we often focus our beliefs on doctrine. God is big enough to guide us deeper into the Word through our mental faculties, but our doctrinal emphasis sometimes reifies the intellectually expressed dimensions of faith. Belief is not about "being right." Belief is an anchor for the Word. Again, these areas of our lives where our heads have left our hearts behind might be where we are being invited to open ourselves up to Lectio and a deeper kind of knowing and learning.

A domestic dimension of learning is also often present in philosophical conversations. Few were better at this—bridging the academic with the domestic, religious ideas with intimate spiritual encounter—than St. Bonaventure. Being an educator at the University Paris helped him talk to us from that experience and bring us into an understanding of ways of coming to know. He was brilliant in his work in the area of philosophy and theology—two sciences not yet so delineated as to seem separate, as people then were simultaneously coming to know both the world and their Creator.

Bonaventure, 800 years ago and today, invites us to multiple ways of knowing and coming to know without diminishing the value of *ratio* and *intellectus* processes—our rational and intellectual faculties. There is a legend that Bonaventure, who was born while St. Francis was still alive, was healed by Francis's presence when he was a sick child. Bonaventure similarly spoke from a beautifully subjective place that today invites us to come alive as the persons we are—to engage with others with fuller ways of coming to know. We have needed, since then, one form or another of renewal. We need to return to a contemporary expression of St. Francis's charism and Christ's presence for him and to all of us. The simplest of things deserves our attention. We begin to see this if we let our awareness of grace permeate everything. Something here, something now, deserves a wakeful eye and an open heart, which inspires our readiness to act out of a place of beauty.

Bonaventure found vibrancy even in the things we might find repetitive, mundane, or redundant. Music, in this sense, might help us learn about the evolving non-redundancy of God. Classical music is often built on a theme that is repetitive, developed over and over through scale and different instruments. We find this in other forms of music, certainly contemporary music. The familiarity is almost part of its pleasure. Its theme returns and deepens, almost as the snow in the woods as December moves to January. It lends comfort and ease to us while we also have an expectation or wonder about what might be next. A baby's cry might wake you from your sleep, but it also invites you into the wonder of your life. A microwaved meal stirs gratitude within your soul. The drive to work you make five times a week becomes an opportunity for silence, prayer, or singing like a fool to the radio.

Almost everything becomes a *scola*—the Latin root where "scholarship" and "school" come from—this gathering of scholars or learners. As you probably have learned yourself, a good teacher remains a student. We linger, looking for what we long for. Life itself becomes ours again. Like a schoolyard merry-go-round, it might drop us off a bit dizzy, but we are grounded nonetheless.

We've been unfortunately trained to go for the meaning, which is to say the idea before the image. In Lectio, we intentionally open the book and reverence its being, which is ready for us to read. Readers become participants. As Thich Nhat Hanh will tell us later (see the final section of Part I), meaning did not first begin in language as we know it, but rather in the forest and in our need for paper that has converged in multiple ways and, together—with the hard work of people in mills and printeries and those who shape words and write books—Lectio is formed again and again, quite literally up from the earth.

Everything has a voice by at least its presence. When the chickadees chirp outside my window, I might not understand the specifics of their communication, yet I understand at times that they are hungry. I understand that they are not afraid of me because they come hungry to be fed out of my hand.

There is a sequential reality of learning that is true about Lectio. It is not repetitive, rather rhythmic at its core. It is always new; yet it might seem repetitive if simply approached as a spiritual task. We gather in a tent that is the Word, and the pole of the tent is Christ. Yet tents are made to move and be mobile; to be put up for a time for a circus or for a family on vacation or during a national disaster. Nonetheless, the structure passes, in some sense, yet also remains in the memory of people who gathered, nurtured, and were cared for in the tent around the pole. It is opening. It is circular. It is unfolding. And it is fundamental to all learning. We return to the question, "What was that again?" over and over, for the answers we hear are always new. In our rush to gain knowledge, sometimes we try to hear and understand everything all at once. But sometimes what we're learning is so full and dense, we can't grasp it all at once. That's why it's good to take life and learning at a slower pace, to not use the clock as a measurement, and to not use our fact-based knowing as a measurement. We are participating in something as sacred as Lectio.

How many times have you risked taking a few steps outside on a cold January night without a jacket and caught glimpse of the stars that have been there all your life? Would you risk it again? Are you willing to pick up a Scripture you've read all your life and risk it becoming new to you? Is there still something of a child in us that would stay outdoors, finding the warmth in the cosmos itself? The cosmos is here and everywhere and humbly invites our attention. If we might reverse the old line from the great Bill Murray, nothing is the "same old, same old." It is an exciting time when we begin to understand this reality.

Coming to know God by reading our lives and our experiences opens us up rather than closes us in. As Paula D'Arcy says, "God comes to us disguised as our life." We are realizing that there is more to "coming to know"—ways that are not solely reliant on the dominion of educational institutions but are indeed human practices; ancient understandings about the nature of being human. Shakespeare famously said, "All the world's a stage," and I would echo this notion and say that "All the world's a classroom." The world—our earth, everyone and everything, the cosmos—is a "living book." It is all sacred Scripture. But you might have to come upon this insight yourself for the reading to begin.

It is one of the deep, rich insights we have from Bonaventure, who lets us know that if we wish to read sacred texts, we should also turn to the created order and learn from the other creatures that are sharing the world with us. They are speaking from their very core, their hearts of being. Out of images and figures, language (and religion) were coming to be.

We are learning there is more to read. There will always be more to read! Robert Bellah's work comes to a wonderful, rich, and subtle completion in his book *Religion in Human Evolution: From the Paleolithic to the Axial Age*. Bellah helps us be humbled by the fact that long before there were words, there was meaning and the search for finding ways to communicate finding food and caring for one another. Religious images, artifacts, and "texts" helped people develop and move. "Evolution" is such a wonderful word for awakening to what is already woven together yet progressing.

At the end of Francis's life, near Clare's community where Francis had written his Canticle of the Creatures, his brothers came to him in the garden and told him that the bishop and the *podestà* were fighting and that the mayor had placed guards outside the bishop's home. So, Francis wrote a new line for the end of the canticle about reconciliation and forgiveness. The brothers went to the palace of the bishop, where people were gathered, and sang the canticle with that new line. You can feel the power of peacemaking in simple words.[42] His Canticle of the Creatures is a cosmological celebration—a banquet of beauty, seen and sung by a man almost blind, who loved creatures and understood that Creation invites us to love one another. His way of coming to know was to listen and then to sing.

COMMUNAL LECTIO

Part of the reason for this book is quite simple: when some of what we refer to as "the church" as an institution seems unable to move with us, the Word of God remains alive and active and is totally transportable. Have you ever been part of a "movement" whether spiritual or political? Or are you active in the shift within the politics of our time? The Word of God came not so much to transport us *out* of such a world but to help us begin to "read" and "be real" in this world. As we move between people and places, the primary movement is always within ourselves, stirred by the Spirit and stories.

Every year, we take the Word on the road, and the Word takes *us* on the road, as we lead groups around the country in the practice of Lectio. As I write this amidst a global pandemic, when many of us are detached from our spiritual communities, I'm reminded how each of us must take Lectio on the road of our lives. There has long been the tendency to parse our own lives into "sacred" and "secular," yet the pandemic has reminded us that we are always being invited to create new rhythms centered in the Word. The Word of God can be read everywhere, is food for everyone, and sits on the table in the universe. So much that seems like it might contradict actually comes together in the Word.

What is your religious practice? Religious practices shifted drastically in 2020. But practices have *already* been shifting the last half-century, especially after Vatican II, as fewer and fewer people are, as the Irish say, "darkening the door of the church." Large historic cathedrals and great monastery churches stand almost empty all across Europe. A sense of spiritual malaise was almost an epidemic before the pandemic. But could we think of this "challenge" more like children? Could we consider where the light is still on and how we might create circles of light rather than curse what we perceive as darkness?

In the United States, the Catholic Church has also been in a quandary, trying to rediscover its place in culture and society. Lectio invites us, as educators, as spiritual directors, as people, to read the "signs of the times" and teach in a way that addresses the world in which we live. God is not quiet or silent, but God certainly is *in* silence.[43]

It has been a great pleasure over the years to travel around the country visiting alumni and leading them in Lectio. We might call it "Lectio on the Road," or, as it has become known over time, "Mountain on the Road." We go to various cities where there is a base of alumni, friends, or others who invite us to, literally, circle up and settle in. Our "traveling circus" consists of a group of students, myself, another friar, and the Director of our Alumni Services. Our role is to offer hospitality and serve the needs of those gathering with us. We receive and honor their trust in leading them into a time of prayer, reflection, *conversatio*, and the opening of the Scriptures in a rich Lectio format.[44] Our "On the Road" ministry has grown and matured in various ways over the last fifteen years and has fostered rich settings for vocational decisions and relationship resolutions, almost without our knowing. This is the way Lectio often works. The micro-church model incubates members for larger communities renewing themselves.

We have circled up outside. We have gathered in comfortable lounges and living rooms. We have met in bare-bones basement rooms in metal folding chairs. Even in this dank space, the quiet is so enriching. We always make space by moving chairs and tables to create an open area, not unlike a bird nesting that finds in the vicinity of its chosen site elements that will be able to "hold the eggs" and foster the coming to life of that which is within the eggs. At the heart of Lectio is treasuring each person as a "hearer of the Word," not idolizing the site or the process. Communal Lectio is about entering the process *to* treasure the person, not make ideas more important than people. The Word of God is the nest—the home in which we return. College students in particular, many of whom grew up compartmentalizing their lives from religion, learn a rich lesson about Lectio and its transportability.

In case you want to take "Lectio on the road" of your life, learning about our tradition will be helpful. No matter where we gather, we set up a small table in the center. We place a piece of art on the table for reflection and a candle recalling baptism. We also place the Bible beside last year's "traveling Easter candle," a pewter bowl, and a pitcher. It is true that you don't need candles, bowls, pitchers, or even sacred Scripture, for that matter, to foster a Lectio experience, but we have found that symbols help to inspire the spiritual imagination, invite those in the room into presence, and cultivate attention and intention. Are there symbols you could place on your desk or dashboard or table that might help you cultivate intention to read the Word throughout your day?

As people arrive and settle in their chairs in a circle around a table, we move into introductions. The youth lead us. In this is its own symbol: in Lectio, we are to become more open, receptive, and childlike, as a student might be. We then light the Easter candle. Our college students set the tone with a warm welcome, often sharing a Scripture, devotional, or personal story. Their transparency invites each person to enter the room on a deeper level: body, soul, and spirit. This simple beginning invites people who might otherwise have been strangers into the sacred nature of the moment. We lead each other further into *conversatio* by trusting each other. Lectio, in a communal sense, is about mutual leadership—the trusting of one another so that we learn and experience the leadership of Christ in our midst. The vulnerability of God in Christ invites us to be vulnerable as well.

After introductions, one of our leaders invites us into a period of silence and stillness—a meditative and contemplative time. A verse from Psalm 46 is then read aloud:

Be still and know that I am God.

Be still and know that I am.

Be still and know.

Be still.

Be.

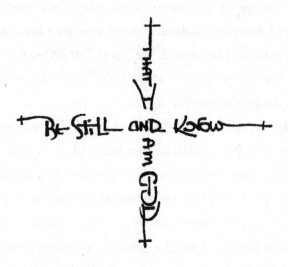

After allowing ourselves to *be* held by this Word, lifted up by the light, treasuring the silence, an opening begins to happen, ever so gently, among us. We discover that we are learning how to listen just by sitting together. We are indeed in solitude while in community. As we come out of silence, we are more alert, able to hear with our hearts.

A song, "There is a Light," written by our friend, Fr. Cyprian Consiglio, OSBCam, a Camaldoli monk on Big Sur, is played. We pour water from a pitcher into a basin. This grounds us in the movement of Grace, bringing us close to the earth and the earth close to us with these earthen images. As we pour the pitcher, we remember our baptisms while listening to Consiglio's beautiful song based on Revelation 7:17: "For the Lamb at the center of the throne will be their shepherd; 'he will lead them to springs of living water.' 'And God will wipe away every tear from their eyes.'" Listening to the song guides us deeper into listening to the water.

No matter where we are, whether it be a church room or a university lounge or someone's home, there is something both ordinary and exceptional about coming alive into the space, where we know Lectio will be central. We "tented" together for a while as itinerants. We have chosen to let the Word shape us; to be the core, the center, the axle of our day and life.

In the ancient practice of Lectio, one would come into a room, church, temple, desert area, or mountain place. *In situ* are Latin words for "in place." The place itself is known and experienced as holy, and so the holy place welcomes us into holiness. One might sense a door or gate there, and this would remind us of Jesus in John's Gospel saying, "I am the gate." So, even in our entering we are journeying further into life, even if felt obscurely, with Christ. Communal Lectio is a simple time of opening, blessing, and sharing with our hearts, as we are tendered by the trust, silence, sense of darkness, and call to the initiation. We help introduce one another to a slower pace, to an easier way of being quiet. The quiet is a passing through the gate. A liberating notion always begins to arise: *"We are one family now."*

MULTI-DIMENSIONALITY AND RELATIONALITY

It is especially clear with Pope Francis writing his letters *Laudato Si'* and *Fratelli tutti* that if we are to be partners in shaping a "new heaven" and a "new earth" we need to learn how to "read" the earth and the heavens. All of creation is both good and a gift from a generous Creator. We must de-colonize our sense of how we value the world, and by that I mean that we must strive to see the earth in its plentitude with all its creatures as they are, as "sisters and brothers," not as only by the way *we* value them as useful.[45] The challenge with dimensionality is that we often, with our labels, cultivate division. Nationalism, for example, can be a separatist movement.

Another word related to "de-colonizing" might be "de-commodifying." Each calls for a discipline to help us regain a radical truth of a familial relationship, a common origin. Our interconnectedness is most noted in our weaving of stories, in art, and in dance. Lectio becomes a liberating way of seeing. Consider the elements of creation—how they have come into our lives and we into theirs. Fire and water and air, for example, have always been important. But we have "thing-ified" them. As Thomas Merton wrote in his essay "Rain and the Rhinoceros":

Let me say this before rain becomes a utility that they can plan and distribute for money. By "they" I mean the people who cannot understand that rain is a festival, who do not appreciate its gratuity, who think that what has no price has no value, that what cannot be sold is not real, so that the only way to make something *actual* is to place it on the market. The time will come when they will sell you even your rain. At the moment it is still free, and I am in it. I celebrate its gratuity and its meaninglessness.[46]

It was likely early humans who began to realize fire was useful. But it was also mysterious. It's hard to think back to who we might have been then, but, remember, we were people without language, arriving with principles. Then, we likely realized fire had a power of its own and therefore had a respect for it. Many native people's beliefs had a similar understanding of the elements, a posture of wonder and humility for whatever it was that came out of the earth.

People who lived on this continent before White settlers arrived did not carry the weight of private ownership. Private ownership, in its darkest ways, has led to the enslavement of others, whether at the end of a long series of battles or the desire for commercial conquests that needed labor. A market was created for people to be bought for the further profiting of another. We are in an age of questioning the impact of private ownership—evaluating how it has both harmed and helped our progress as humans. We live in a time that has its own need for "new reading"—a deep form of Lectio.

No wonder our relationships with one another are often transactional—that's how we treat the earth on which we live! I wonder if transaction is where loneliness originates. When we're not in relationship with what is around us, we can feel isolated. Something in us knows that transaction is not a full or complete way of living. Some couples I've met never tried to make the other one the completion of themselves. Their spirituality or sense of God became deepened by the continued incompleteness of their lives.

Much of this rises out of St. Irenaeus's work, which is centered around *covenant*, a sacred relationship. Irenaeus's work, along with that of others, is foundational to the Franciscan notion of "recapitulation"—the completion of all things in Christ. *Caput* means "head" in Latin, and is where we derive other words like "capstone," as in a capstone college course that covers all that has been learned thus far in our particular area of study. Christ is the head, bringing unity and completion to all things, perpetually flowing in "fountain fullness," Bonaventure's great metaphor.

This unfolding truth of God is amazing, isn't it? It can devise a heady or cerebral framework, or we can find it in our place beside us as we walk in the woods. We remember, here, that we are reading relationships. It is not so much about opening a book we need to study but rather what we might call "pleasure reading"—the joy of seeing our sisters and brothers in all their "newness" once more as members of one family. Reading helps us be attentive, to treasure their qualities and gifts. No matter the season, life has us walking somewhere, and we have the opportunity to become more alert to the beauty and wonder of creation around us. Creation is truly brought forth by the hand of God. We see the forest floor, leaf by leaf, or a pond with leaves floating on it, or fish surfacing as swans glide by, and our breath lifts and is taken away and given to us again. All of this is the breath of God who is still breathing into Creation.

You and I become witnesses of life as it is. This becomes one of our core reasons for the transformation of our own hearts and lives. "The eye of the heart"[47] is the place and way of transformation, first transformed by our longing to see clearly as God sees us. We then become witnesses of God's work, and we become witnesses *for* God of our sisters and brothers in creation. We can feel how the simple movement of prayer and meditation and conversation in Lectio naturally moves to relationship and to action. We would become more alert—yes, receptive to beauty—and because of that, more disposed to the needs of others.

Lectio leaves us wondering as we notice remnants—aspects and parts that are not necessarily rationally connected, but somehow dance together. This kind of seeing is fundamental. It is the risky activity of people who assemble around artwork to trust the artist who is assembling it for us, bringing order in some way into the world by bringing us into the view of that artist's understanding of order. This is sometimes portrayed as disorder.

When Bonaventure was exhausted, he tells us in the introduction of his *Itinerarium Mentis in Deum* that he was climbing Mt. La Verna "with a panting spirit." Self-disclosure (first to ourselves) can be an important opening to a time in Lectio. Elements of our Lectio practice ask that we become self-aware and self-present. That does not mean necessarily needing to disclose at that time what we have become alert to, but rather knowing it's the terrain and texture of who we are as we assemble. It is that which receives the reign of the word of God, the water that pours on us. It's the place where things can seep in. It's "how" we find ourselves at this moment in time and see it with our inner senses, as Bonaventure would say, which helps us to be wise about the Word and hear it as it calls us to union.

READING WORLDS IN WORDS

Everyone learns to read at a different pace. For a long time, I was uninterested in reading. I was looking at the world around me but possibly was not disciplined enough to spend time with words on a page. In fact, I was told I might have to stay back in sixth grade. My reading level was only that of fourth grade! Around that time, I remember riding in the car with my father on our way home from downtown Rochester, and he asked me to read to him a few signs and billboards. Something opened up for me on that drive. In being prompted by my father to read, I remember suddenly being fascinated by all I could see around me. He had invited me into awareness. I was less interested in the words on the billboards and signs and more fascinated by all the people on the streets near the buildings and the traffic as it was flowing in the city. I might have struggled to read words, but I was still reading the world and its billboards quietly.

My parents later asked a teacher down the street to help me out. She came by the house one day and matter-of-factly dropped off a couple of books, one of which I remember being a nature-related book called *Along the Santa Fe Trail*. That was sixth grade. At the end of that year, I was reading at an eleventh-grade level and consuming books by the week. Reading words became as real as reading the world had felt that day with my father. Words became a doorway into another world.

My parents taught us that we are a family that reads. During my childhood, it would not have been unusual to see three of us reading in the living room. We felt that the television was an intrusion upon family time and reading time. What is intruding upon your life and the ability to read?

Reading with interest, with the willingness to let words speak to you in the moment—in the immediacy of your life and all that you might be enjoying, enduring, or encountering—adds a deliberate aspect to Lectio. Franciscan Lectio opens out, from reading the words on the page to reading the people among us in the intimacy of our setting, reading the light falling on the page or the wind blowing outside or the cars going by, reading the newspaper and the words and letters, even the typeface! It's all a gift from God to us, this gift of eternally integrating this unconscious desire to see the One—that which is unitive—in the midst of the many.

These days I read texts, which, along with books, are also stones, ideas, sounds, promises, sacred scriptures, presence, and mercy. When Lectio was emerging as a practice among "people of the book," it's important to remember that not many people had books. Books and scrolls were normally held in common places to be shared, though wealthier people had their own books and monasteries had libraries. Books heightened the beauty of the word for us. The words that detailed stories and ideas were of great significance. The recorded word moved from speech and gesture to objective "code"—alphabet configuration on material that had an apparent permanence. The importance of carrying it in our heart indicates a similar kind of permanence.

As you might recall, books (early on) were on more simple materials: skins and rocks and other natural elements. Their own development, in some ways, parallels that of the ability to write—the figures and shapes of alphabets that evolved over time. Prior to books, people had a great capacity for remembering stories and sacred texts, as well as other things. Whole books were held in memory. Often books of the Bible were "held" in the memory of certain people within a community. The expansive memories of people were a great service to those around them.

Thich Nhat Hanh gives us a window into his genius for childlike *in*-sight in his writing about a simple piece of paper. One of Thay's (which means "teacher") primary offerings for us in his book *The Heart of Understanding* is the notion of "inter-being"—the wondrous worlds and interconnectedness we might read in the simplest things, stirring awe and gratitude within our souls. I encourage you to take a little time to do a simple meditation following the reading of this passage. Over and over again, Thay invites us into something that Westerners often find uncomfortable; to take the time to see what really is before us and around us.

If you are a poet, you will see clearly that there is a cloud floating in this sheet of paper. Without a cloud, there will be no rain; without rain, the trees cannot grow; and without trees, we cannot make paper. The cloud is essential for the paper to exist. If the cloud is not here, the sheet of paper cannot be here either. So we can say that the cloud and the paper *inter-are*. "Interbeing" is a word that is not in the dictionary yet, but if we combine the prefix "inter-" with the verb "to be," we have a new verb, inter-be. Without a cloud, we cannot have paper, so we can say that the cloud and the sheet of paper *inter-are*.

If we look into this sheet of paper even more deeply, we can see the sunshine in it. If the sunshine is not there, the forest cannot grow. In fact, nothing can grow. Even we cannot grow without sunshine. And so, we know that the sunshine is also in this sheet of paper. . . .

Suppose we try to return one of the elements to its source. Suppose we return the sunshine to the sun. Do you think that this sheet of paper will be possible? No, without sunshine nothing can be. And if we return the logger to his mother, then we have no sheet of paper either. The fact is that this sheet of paper is made up only of "non-paper elements." And if we return these non-paper elements to their sources, then there can be no paper at all. Without "non-paper elements," like mind, logger, sunshine and so on, there will be no paper. As thin as this sheet of paper is, it contains everything in the universe in it."[48]

This inter-being is core-logic—the very *logos* of Lectio. It is experiential, as we reverently open our hearts in prayer to stillness and begin to listen and let the eye of our heart see again. The inter-relatedness of all of life—as our needs open our imaginations—invites us to see the new heaven and new earth *here*. Thay points the way in simply opening up the life of a piece of paper.

Every thing and everyone comes from God in Christ and returns through the Son in the Spirit to the Father. We hear this in John's Gospel when he says that "no one, nothing is lost that the Father gave me." This wonderful collecting, this drawing in, and, in some real way, recycling of ourselves, is the ongoing fullness that Jesus fosters among us. We are all one in the Word, more awake to this reality thanks to the living, breathing sheet of paper before us. We have been lifted up in the Bread of Life and have the capacity to be food for others. The Word teaches us this. We begin to see that we are not lost. We are gathered, and we are fed.

PART II
CONSIDER

RUMINATING ON THE WORD

"Consider, examine . . . if you suffer with him, you will reign with him, grieving with him, you will rejoice with him."
—ST. CLARE OF ASSISI

"And in the beginning was love. Love made a sphere: all things grew within it; the sphere then encompassed beginnings and endings, beginning and end. Love had a compass whose whirling dance traced out a sphere of love in the void: in the center thereof rose a fountain."
—ROBERT LAX, *"Circus of the Sun"*

"But if you wish to know how these things come about,
ask grace not instruction,
desire not understanding,
the groaning of prayer not diligent reading,
the Spouse not the teacher,
God not man,
darkness not clarity,
not light but the fire that totally inflames and carries us into God."
—ST. BONAVENTURE

*I*n July 1965, my family drove me through northern New Jersey to a Franciscan novitiate for Holy Name Province. It had been about a year since I had decided to become a "monastic style" novice. A contemplative lifestyle gripped my heart: up at five in the morning, in bed by nine in the evening, the whole day planned in brief sections between study, work, prayer, exercise, and almost all of it in grand silence.

My father had been especially proud and supportive of my choice to become a friar, and he had reflected this in almost everything he said weeks before my family dropped me off. As a young boy I had followed him to "First Fridays" and admired how still and quiet he was in church, especially after communion, and how reverent and peaceful he was, even though he was a very animated and emotional man. God, prayer, and family were his joy, as well as his cross.

After our formal ceremony for our reception as novices, I walked my parents (Jake and Fran Riley), my sisters (Patty and Ellen), and my friend (Margee Delaney) to their car. We said goodbye. As I returned to St. Raphael's Novitiate and its large doors closed behind me, it was as if the doors were shutting out the whole world—as indeed they were intended to do.

A few weeks later I was peeling potatoes in silence in our kitchen when a novice and another friar were sent to tell me that our novice master wanted to see me in his office. As I walked into his office, it was as if I sensed nothing was going to be the same again.

The novice master asked me to take a seat, and he looked at me with gentle eyes. "I have to tell you, Frater Daniel Paul, that your father died suddenly yesterday."

I looked at him, unsure of what to say. My feelings and my world were spinning.

"You may go home for the funeral, Frater," he continued, "but an extended visit with your family away from here may break your canonical novitiate."

Though not intentionally insensitive, he was preoccupied with Canon Law and the structuring of religious life. His sense of the structure of novitiate was so top-down, so out-in, that he had real difficulty dealing with something so unexpected—my father's death—which now flooded our novitiate with a reality he hadn't yet contended with either. I had a great deal of affection for my novice master and came to know him even better, especially later in life. He was a shy, kind man, and we were all in a time when the church and church formation programs were about to change. He bore the stress of the pole hitting the fulcrum. So, on that time, and on that day, I knew I had someone who was worried about something other than myself. Though I don't remember being angry, I knew I was left alone in the reality of my dad's death. I have made this mistake in my life as well—a terrible preoccupation with order or preparation, making me far less present to reading the anxieties or sufferings of people whom I might be among.

It was a short visit home, five days with family and close friends. I mostly watched over my mother, who was in a state of shock and helplessness. Our first time together in a long time, my four siblings—Jimmy, Denny, Patty, and Ellen—and I were grasping, each in our own way, at a reality we could not contain while it gripped us.

Within a week, I returned to the novitiate. Those doors closed behind me again, and this time I felt separated and truly alone.

In the months that followed, the sudden and terrible loss for my family remained just as poignant, weighing heavy on my heart and mind. I was awash, alone, and lonely. I was not clear about my feelings at the time. The emotions were new for me. The woods became a sanctuary for me as the shock settled, as I began sifting through the layers and complexities of grief.

One October afternoon I remember going for a walk in my habit and sandals on the novitiate's beautiful grounds on a high hill in North Jersey, then farm country. I had just left our large, square, brick novitiate building, which had a private garden in its middle, reflective of the solitude and seclusion that was offered to all of us. Fields spread around the garden, as well as a beautiful wooded area in the back with trails, including a big horseshoe-shaped trail that entered the woods, circled around, and came back out again into the field. To stand in the midst of hardwoods on those trails—that sacred space that felt so safe and secluded—now was a great comfort.

Dry leaves covered the trail, and the bright blue sky was shining through the trees above. Trees and forests—there is something about the wonder, mystery, and protection of entering into them. This had been one of my greatest joys in my childhood. When troubled or lost, I would jump on my bike and ride it down to the woods. I would find a brook or listen again for Brown Falls or Red Falls or go all the way to the Genesee Gorge. Then, I would return home after a day in the woods to my mother and father. And now I was finding that, even with my father gone, these woods were still another home.

Suddenly, as I walked, a large oak leaf slid between my big toe and the next one, settling in as if it had found its own place, as if Creation and its Creator had found me.

I felt this happen and looked down. I stopped walking, somewhat stunned by the comfort and the character of this encounter. This leaf had become a friend simply by entering in. My toes had caught the leaf, and the leaf had caught me, in an unintentional, subtle way. And as the leaf settled in, it was going to move with me as I walked slowly through the woods.

Now there were the two of us.

Stronger still was the call to stand still, to be quiet for a few moments. Of all the leaves beneath my feet, covering the coursing path ahead, this one spoke for all of them. It seemed to say something about the character and personality—the specificity—of each branch and leaf in this wooded area in which I now stood. A leaf had seemingly "chosen" to join me. It had entered with humility, at my feet, as Jesus does on Holy Thursday, helping me to feel momentarily washed of my grief and troubles, brought into the joy of companionship and the awesomeness of this simple friend. I smiled down through my tears and looked up through the canopy of trees to the azure sky. And it was enough.

LECTIO AND THE SENSES

This day, today, as I write, brings it back again, as the surprise of November sunlight, after a string of gray days, bleeds through my window, warming my living room. The leaves outside glisten in the breeze, their shine multiplied by thin layers of ice. Curled, colorful maple and brown oak leaves reach up toward the autumn sky. Soon they will fall and perhaps find others who walk through our woods. I know that there are no words to name the beauty of that intimate encounter I had decades ago with that oak leaf. An encounter is just that, a naked engagement, especially between two who come beside each other and leave themselves open to being together in some wonderful and graced way. That walk was my time with the oak leaf, which was free to go when it wished, but stayed with me on my way.

Prayer begins in us when we have barely begun to pray. As in Ephesians, often quoted by Bonaventure and other Franciscans, we almost desperately begin to "see with the eye of our heart," or, as the Little Prince said, "only with the heart can one see rightly." Are you tired by now of seeing that Ephesians passage quoted? What if you allowed it to become new for you as I continue to introduce it "as if for the first time"?

There are many ways of seeing—and not only through the eyes, but also through our other senses: The alertness of a toe that would feel something come close, the beauty of the breeze, the crackle of the leaves, and all of this converging in a simple encounter. All these senses long to come alive to what is alive, even though, yes, it was autumn and this leaf had died, fallen already to the floor of a forest. Ironically, it was a leaf, something that had fallen, that lifted me up; it had brought me up from a place in which I had been entrenched, deeper probably than I even realized. It was seeing this without seeing it and finding it without searching for it, that began to become a real entrance into contemplation for me.

Nothing is *only* inanimate. Everything, when we "have eyes to see" and read life in its fullness—its faithfulness to its Creator—is more full than we first find it. If we open our eyes a bit more, we begin to find the quality and capacity of others to communicate or to at least receive us beside them, to somehow carry what we call presence and sometimes even apply personality (like the tenderness of the leaf) to what, up until now, we spoke of as inanimate.

This "naming" as we walk through the garden of our life, not unlike Adam and Eve in Eden, rises out of Lectio—our ongoing activity of reading, both with and within the activity of the Creator that we read about and hear about.

Yahweh who continues to be faithful.

The One who sent his Son among us.

This is the One who has blessed us with all our other creaturely companions as we walk with our "sister, Mother Earth," as St. Francis would say, and "our common home," as Pope Francis helps us know.

As I have noted elsewhere, far from playing with pantheism, this is a type of pan-*en*-theism—God present through the very Spirit and sustainer of everything, as Colossians tells us. This isn't straining the Word, but it helps to nuance the truth so that the quality of being remains. We hear this reflected so richly in the writings of St. Bonaventure and others before him and marvelous contemporary theologians such as Ilia Delio.[49]

How might we begin to awaken our senses again if we have been stuck in our head or our systems of commodifying? Bonaventure, whose work is still being uncovered and discovered, takes time to help us know the importance of all our senses, not just our intellect. We might say these are the "inner" and "outer" senses—the space in which you and I emerge as full human beings, when we become more embodied and alert. The ability to feel and see and hear is more than just an emotional reality, and certainly more than just a rational one. People are drawn to Bonaventure's work, I believe, because of his cosmic sense of things, aesthetic theology, and his spherical awareness (which was later stretched out in a spiral by Teilhard de Chardin[50]), all of which present a certain challenge to linear thinking in a pragmatic world. He was multi-dimensional, understanding a more expanded spectrum without naming the colors and, like other mystics, a quantum thinker before we had the word "quantum" for physics—in fact, before we had the science we now call physics. Yet, he was very clear in his practice of life, longing, seeking, journeying, and opening his soul to God.

In the prologue of *The Soul's Journey into God*, Bonaventure awakens us with language we're not always comfortable with when he talks about the groaning of our hearts in prayer. Through his own suffering, he counsels us how "to read," learn, and come to wisdom.

"First, therefore, I invite the reader
to groans of prayer
through Christ crucified,
through whose blood,
we are cleansed from the filth of vice—
so that he not believe that reading is sufficient without unction,
speculation without devotion,
investigation without wonder,
observation without joy,
work without piety,
knowledge without love,
understanding without humility,
endeavor without divine grace,
reflection as a mirror without divinely inspired wisdom."

In elegant imagery, he is encouraging us to turn from *ratio*—only a primarily rational or intellectual approach—and instead open up to a richer experience, what Franciscans might identify as more fully incarnational openness. This is a truly visceral encounter with the created order. Lectio Divina is an encounter, an event that totally engages us, all of us—both our inner and outer senses.

St. Irenaeus (AD 130–202), even more ancient than Bonaventure (1221–1274), offers us a sound picture of our place within the beauty of the work God has done and continues to do. He once wrote a commentary on Genesis where we receive from him a hopeful sense of our coming to be as human beings. The first garden, Eden, is the eternal *paradiso*. We were never taken away from it because that garden is Christ. The gift of contemplation—being awestruck and aware of this unity and community of all things—comes implanted and imprinted in each of us. It will show itself, this munificence, as we stop, look, listen, walk, or sit. We realize again and again we are in the garden!

On that day walking through the woods, I saw what it was to hear, and I began to hear what it meant to see with both eyes. This kind of intimate encounter is in the Scriptures and especially in John's literature: to see *out* from *within* as we open ourselves to what is *around* us, to those we are among, and to those who might be beyond us here. In other words, we have, right here, in this moment, an experience with the expanse of the cosmos—not just the knowledge that it is out there, but that it is also at hand. We begin to open from within to see what is beside us and beyond us. The prophet Jeremiah's words ring out, "You are in our midst, LORD, your name we bear: do not forsake us!"[51]

The brown, orange, crinkled, and smooth-skinned leaf did not invade my sandal or mess up my walk. It led me into our relationship that was already there (here). Somehow, the leaf told me I was not alone in my loneliness. I was standing in solitude and solidarity with other creatures who were also passing. It humbly, endlessly spoke of the others near with no worry about being lost in the shuffle of "the many." It rested in between my toes and let me know that we are all at home here. Our senses open us to the One who abides within each of us, this strikingly true domestic God. The One who dwells in our very home is not asleep but rather ready for us to awake. Our amazing senses—feeling, seeing, tasting, smelling, touching—open our hearts to perhaps be touched by a leaf that seems to see us coming down the path.

We are all companions to one another. Our senses are windows and gateways. Ideas and thoughts about all these things are, by nature, somewhat static. Lectio invites us to occasionally sit beside this other way of coming to know: through what Bonaventure describes as the senses.

Experiential learning calls out for practices and habits of reflection and integration. But we arrived at this truth, not through our intellect first, but through our senses. It is not *intellectus* or *ratio* only at work, but it *is* encounter and engagement. It is being here (not thinking about being here) that has us understand what *is* here and where *here* is. We might then pause for a moment and say this is one of the beauties of Lectio and its sensual contribution. We often think of our senses, or at least I do, as a subset of everything else. But let's take a break and have a fun approach to them. Along with the joy, pleasure, pain, and confounding of our senses is a wonderful capacity for them to be "teachers."

Intimacy. What does this word mean to you? It is one of those words that might leave us breathless. Or it might increase our heart rate as we light a candle or pour a glass of wine or set a table in our heart. Intimacy is more than romance, though there may very well be romance in the most ecstatic and mystical intimacies. We hear it in some of our great mystics of the East and West.

Intimacy is felt quite differently for each of us. Nonetheless, one of the things we live for and breathe for—that our hearts beat most for—is to share intimacy (with someone). Why? Because it is multi-dimensional and multidirectional. Intimate knowing embraces human complexity. It stirs us. It holds high and low feelings. Our look for intimacy can be both romantic and frustrating. It might draw us in or revel us. It might frighten us or have us wish to abandon this part of our journey. Some of us have been so wounded that we do our best not to become intimate.

This is not meant to be a short piece on sex education, rather a fuller sense of the erotic. *Eros,* as the Greeks spoke of it and we know it, is a wonderful yearning—with all that we are—to be one with the other. Many would talk about intimacy almost as an "eternal return." Think of it in this radical, spiritual way—of a creature returning to its creator with a longing and true passion to be with the One who has made us. We find this in the great love poetry of the Psalms and in Wisdom. Proverbs is so suggestive of what is really, first, erotic, though our modern minds tend to focus on what we think of as sexually suggestive. We get the sense in this sacred literature that we are moving toward eros and sexuality to find mutuality in us again.

We long to be one. We often will go out of our way to "climb the highest mountain" and be with the one in whom we long for intimacy. As St. Augustine wrote, "Our hearts are restless, until they can find rest in you." *Ruach*, a feminine word in Hebrew, used to name the wind or breath over the waters at the time of creation, is a wonderful word of engagement, involvement, and entering *into* and *with* "the other." All of this suggests some of the descriptiveness of the erotic. God is love and is always love and is one with all of it!

We might also consider the wisdom of Mary Magdalene, who, as scholars are more apt to tell us in recent centuries, was not a "lady of the streets." She was a woman at Jesus's table and at his Cross. She was a disciple, a very good friend along the way. Then there is Jesus's mother, Mary, the flower and rose who blossomed in holy virginity, whose openness to intimacy led to giving birth to the Incarnate Lord. She received God through the Holy Spirit's announcement and was "filled with the Holy Spirit," as we know. This radical intimacy is not something we stand back and look at, my friends. This indeed is the intimacy we are invited to enter into; a path we too are called to follow. We know and celebrate the fact that our Christian history began with God's Spirit and a woman who said yes.

I'm always stirred by these lines in Psalm 31:8–9 (emphasis mine): "I will rejoice and be glad in your mercy, once you have seen my misery, and gotten to know the distress of my soul. You will not abandon me into enemy hands, but will set my feet in a *free and open space*." This "free and open space" where we ask God to set our feet is the passage beside the Christ, the firstborn of all Creation. Creature by creature, we walk in a closeness, which is to say in the freedom of intimacy. We are waiting for this very close and personal involvement with the cosmos and its creator.

In Bob Lax's "Circus of the Sun," with a type of cosmic grounding, Lax closes a particularly beautiful scene of waking in the morning with the other workers of the circus, opening the flap of his tent, and "rising and coming into the field." This, I believe, is a particular Christic acclamation. Lectio invites us into this spaciousness, this "free and open space" of listening to God's Word, having been through turmoil and difficulties. We assimilate it, or we chew it over; we mull it over and take it in. It takes us in. This is the intimacy of Lectio.

THE CORE OF LECTIO

Lectio flips our most accepted way of "coming to know" on its head, constantly reminding us that our library is larger than the books on our shelves, or the shelves at our institutions. Our systems of learning still get stuck around conveying or measuring facts and have not always led to truth telling. They have not always prepared people to reflect in heartfelt ways to integrate oneself and the needs of others. Lectio asks us to read everything and never leave the book that is before us. We read not to "get through something" but live through it and bring others into this cosmic experience of Christ, one day at a time. The Word is living in our midst, even when we are used to containing things. Abundance isn't about acquiring things; it's about receiving all of life. The abundance of the Word is ongoing, and as partners in Lectio, we read life as it grows.

Franciscan poverty, as I understand it, is realizing that so much has been given to us, even when whatever feels loose on the edges of our lives tries to convince us otherwise. In Lectio, this "inner poverty" (as Thomas Merton called it) can become a gateway to spiritual abundance—the kind of abundance we read about in John 17, when Jesus says to his followers, "All I have is yours, and all you have is mine," or in the Parable of the Prodigal Son when the father says to the eldest, "You are ever with me, and all that I have is yours." Inner poverty—finding oneself vacuous and empty—often feels like we are spinning out of control, but in Lectio, we might become aware of all that has already been given to us. As Zachary Hayes unfolded his Christology so wonderfully in his book *The Hidden Center*, the hidden center of everything—the sphere that Bonaventure talks about—is Christ.[52]

At the center of their lives Christians celebrate a God who wholeheartedly gave "Himself" undividedly for us, pouring out his heart and all he was. His "sweat was like drops of blood falling to the ground" in the anguish he experienced in the Garden of Gethsemane. Blood flowed from his side, palms, feet, and head the next day when he was crucified. This would be a sign of the stream that flows from the temple and the new covenant or union that is the heart of God in Christ, his son and our Lord.

Several years ago, a quote from William Blake was given to me. It was already framed because it had hung in the home of Mary Daly, a neighbor of Bob Lax, who was a close friend of Thomas Merton's. It was Lax who brought Merton to Olean and then to St. Bonaventure University at a transitional time in Merton's life.[53] The quote read, "All that is without, though it seems to be, is within."

When I was a student at St. Bonaventure in the early 1960s, meeting Fr. Irenaeus and beginning to read Merton, I was considering being a doctor. One day a Franciscan sister, Sr. Rose Francis, emerged from the spiral staircase, up from the stacks of our library. She smiled at me and said, "Bill, I was looking for you. I have a prayer for you." She handed me a prayer card. On one side it said, *"Creation is the flower of infinite poverty,"*[54] and on the other side was a beautifully written note that she would pray for me. She said, with deep blue eyes looking into mine, "Have you ever thought of becoming a Franciscan?"

Have you ever had someone call you out to a possible path in life? Maybe they perceived a movement or gift in you that they read on your face or in your life. We read each other and might lend to one another a sense of direction.

The sister who gave me the note was right. Creation *is* the flower of infinite poverty. The bounty of all that is ours, that is poured out here for us, came forth from this God who pours everything out from the origin of God's incarnate self: the Word. This is part of the experience of Lectio: to read and listen to this ongoing activity of the God who will not relent in letting us know of God's love and mercy. Creation becomes the flower of infinite poverty when we understand poverty is self-emptying as we learn to love, as we learn to see our connectedness.

Though disputed as a quote from Chief Seattle, a native chief around the time that White settlers were invading and occupying native land as if it were property, these lines are often quoted at the end of his beautiful speech: "This we know. All things are connected like the blood that unites one family. All things are connected."

Lectio, at its core, is connecting. The inner dynamic of *conversatio* is precisely the dynamic activity of the Word enfleshing itself between two or more hearers so that, with them, there is a rapport, an engagement, a deepening of communion and understanding leading to action. This graced encounter is held in the arms of the God who is always speaking to us, always heightening the fact that we are not only connected but that we are one.

When Pope Francis offered us *Laudato si'* (Praise be, you, my Lord, for per [through] all you have made), which had the subtitle, "On care for our common home," we were reminded of Chief Seattle's timeless words. We are once more invited to know the *all*—to read it in the stars and in the rivers and in the snow; to read it on the plains as the grass moves in the wind; to read it in the small and defenseless, the terminally ill, and the first day of a baby's life. The universe is vast and all—so immense that you and I have an opportunity to encounter it as it emerges in us and around us.

One morning during Mass, right before we received the Eucharist, we saw a deer with two fawns pass by the chapel. As we made our way down the hill for brunch, someone observed that the mother had left one of the fawns behind. This little animal, possibly only a few hours old, damp with her mother's fluids, was curled up under a tree and lay there with its large, soft, doe eyes open, but seemingly full of sadness. It may have been the first day of light for her eyes, and yet they were already dark for fear. And here she was. Where was her mother? Not near, it seemed. The fawn was vulnerable, with its own heart beating, a heart somehow set by the same Creator who called me and the few of us who stood by her there. In that quiet time, I felt a sense of helplessness.

Someone later reminded me that the mother often leaves the fawn to distract humans or other creatures who might be near. You might know that the fawn has no fragrance—no detectible aroma for their predators. The mother departs in order to clear the way. She often stands off hidden and watches. She is a sentinel for her newborn.[55]

We went back later, and the fawn was gone.

There seemed to be no sign of a tussle or problem there.

God, too, "has left us in the world" but is not far off and is always present to us. Isn't it interesting that in an encounter like this we often are flooded by worry and images of tragedy? Possibly, your life has been filled with the latter, but God is always here and returns to us—and probably more often than our imaginations would reach. Seeing the fawn's helplessness called us into life—into darkness and pain, mystery and joy, poverty and connectedness with creation— as Life reached out to life. Our connectedness with all things, as St. Paul directs us, helps us find our wholeness in the living Word. The Word has no borders. As Leonard Bernstein wrote in his masterpiece *MASS*, the Word of God cannot be "chained"—though we may often tame it even before we hear it.[56] Bernstein uses this passage as an introduction to a life witnessing to justice and peacemaking. We find our unencumbered wholeness in the Word. The Word is unexpected. It is complex. It stirs an array of emotions and sensations within our hearts that awakens our connectedness with all things. As Bernstein and Stephen Schwarz write in the libretto: *"For the Word was at the birth of the beginning. / It made the heavens and the earth and set them spinning. / And for several million years / it's endured all our forums and fine ideas. / It's been rough but it appears to be winning!"*

STOP, LOOK, LISTEN

When I was a young boy, I learned a simple, but lifelong lesson: the importance of "stopping, looking, and listening." You probably learned this as well. It is one of the most primary lessons for life and safety, as well as entering into the world. Especially in this age—when there is so much violence, division, and, yes, unfortunately, fear mongering—this simple conscious movement of stopping, looking, and listening can help us to re-center ourselves and begin to see things clearly once again.

You and I, as human beings made in the image of God, are called into the profound safety of a God who has loved us tenderly. One of the great ancient Latin words is *attendre*, which means to "be attentive" or "give over our attention." We also see this idea called out in other wonderful religions in the world. An ongoing notion from perennial traditions is that the way we begin to see, know, and be is to *read* reality, which first involves adopting this attentive stance.

"Stance" might mean sitting, resting in place, or lying down as a harbor for reflection. Stance is whatever the bodily habit is that pauses us to be attentive. Whether it's chakra-focused or breath-attentive, whether it's a mantra, a mandala, a moment, a moon (but, as Asian wisdom might say, not the finger pointing toward it!), it all calls for attention. We stand in our attentiveness in the light of the moon, seeing by its aid, but not pointing at it as if to say, "Look!" It's no good to be preoccupied with stance, with technique.

In the Judeo-Christian tradition, this idea, in my opinion, is epitomized in Moses's encounter with the burning bush. As some writers have noted quite nicely, "everything is a burning bush," or, as Thomas Merton says, "the gate of heaven is everywhere." I love the story of the burning bush because it is so human and relatable. It invites me to see the divine at-one-ment, which, in its first portrayal, is not tied to our failure or sinfulness. Here is Moses, busy in his responsibilities, working for his father-in-law, Jethro, caring for his goats. Moses understands what it's like to be stressed, to feel pressure, and to be worn out with the day-to-day duties of life. But then all of a sudden he hears or feels—and then senses—something of the divine in a bush. The bush is speaking to Moses, calling out to him, and inviting him to be attentive.

For me, this is one of the most sacred moments in all of human history and, though one might understand the story as a myth or speak of it as a non-historical event, it converges the stories of not only the Israelite people, but others who encounter a God who is no longer confined to a mountaintop or in a cloud or on a temple shelf. A God who is no longer distant but is instead immediate to us. A God who is accessible. A God who is relatable. *Immanuel.*

It continues to be the Bible-on-the-dorm-room-desk moment I experienced as a student at St. Bonaventure. There is no veil after all. There is no division. God—the naked, poor, joyful, and present Christ who Francis came to see, and as he became more attentive, to follow and to serve—is to be experienced here and now.

Those who have studied the Hebrew language will also recognize that when the bush—the *angel*—announces to Moses the presence of "YHWH" (the Tetragrammaton), it is not the word itself or the letters that are most interesting, but rather the breath that comes to us between those Hebrew characters. In Latin, *con* means "with" and *sonants* means "sound." Consonants go with the sound, which is to say they go with the breath. Consonants are here—YHWH—humble caretakers of the mysterious space between them through which God, who is breath, comes and goes as God pleases. The burning bush that Moses encounters is a living, breathing, and eternal presence that has never left anything that has been formed and shaped. If this suggests anything of the amazement of the Almighty, try attempting to translate it into English, and sit for a while remembering that the breath between these pillars of Hebrew characters, the arriving of God, is the very one who says "I will never leave." It is what St. John called the "Word." Moses is being called to "read" what the One has fully revealed; to focus on this blazing experience and be transformed by it, as all things are, or, as we would say, transformed in Christ.

When I was on retreat at a Catholic meditation center near Tucson, Arizona, and began sitting in meditations, the spiritual leaders there talked about "spaciousness"—the practice of being open, waiting for, and receiving the light. Moses's encounter asks us to be willing to step outside the lines of the paths we are on—though listening deeply and being attentive to the One who calls out to us. We might feel a draw to go somewhere. We might be listening and looking to what is unfolding in front of us. We might have to stop a bit, for a moment, in order to consider what is going on in our minds as something of a burning bush speaks to us and invites us in to an experience of presence.

God is immediate to us, not allusive. God is not like a genie, available to us at our bidding, but rather at God's own self-giving. The Word that we encounter in Lectio is a gift from God, and it's historically rooted in the encounter of Moses with Yahweh. This becomes an archetypical encounter echoed down to the very person of Jesus, the Christ. Moses did not "go get" Yahweh, nor does Yahweh withhold the wholeness of God's being from Moses. Rather, both are wonderfully exposed and expressed in this outdoor moment, on a path on a mountain, when work is put aside.

Think of the intimate scope of this. It is so wonderful, rich, and vulnerable. And Yahweh models that vulnerability, revealed with a humble bush, and unfolding a name to Moses: "I Am who I Am" or "As who I Am I shall be with you," or "I am here, and I will be with you" or "I will never be anywhere else but beside you." Even in these translations, we can see that words fall short, unable to fully unpack the meaning that arose out of another culture and language, thousands of years ago. Lectio takes us in, through and beyond the words themselves. This is an incredible intersection—the story of the God who is here, not aloof or distant. The mountain God, who is on the path beside us, is a pure gift. We learn how to give that gift of presence to others, just as God does for us.

WORD, MAN, WORD

I remember hearing a simple expression a couple decades ago that rose, as I recall, from the West Coast and moved East. When I first heard it, it rang out like a great bell of freedom. Ringing out of vibrant Black communities that have been socially oppressed by a history of racism, not unlike what the Word has experienced, that expression was simply this: "*Word, man, word.*" Said with heart and soul, perhaps right after hearing a profound word of truth, it struck me. "Word, man, word," meaning that there is a connection, a relatedness with deep and real meaning. The Word is power, and we know power in the action of the Word.

The pauses between the words are just as important as the phrase. The quiet that is there is the quiet we hear when the Word emerges, like a silent sunrise with the Christ, who is the Son, bringing us a new day. It is for us to open our eyes to this. It is God reaching out from within each one of us and shaping something new. It is a power that is that intimate, immediate to us, and able to be expressed, that will make a difference now—if we allow it to be free and to free us.

I'm moved by how the Black community has been able to take other words and phrases and make them their own and turn them back to those who want to listen. Freedom is first radicalized from within the heart of a person, as we have seen in Gandhi, King, Mandela, and Sojourner Truth. Each has their own legacy for our own hearts. Each might awaken in us what longs to come awake. "Woke," before it became politicized, is similar, essentially meaning, "Now you're reading something new and starting to see in a new way."

As we write this book, people once again are longing for truth— for the truth of our history, of all of our people, and of freedom. Decades after I heard that crisp, clear expression—"Word, man, word," a radical truth—I have had to face into the reality of racism again in myself and others around me, as if "for the first time." All sorts of things have happened to our country, some historic atrocities and others wonderful demonstrations that would invite us to know that Black lives matter. The Word did become flesh. And it not only came among us but lives among us, beside us, and we are still finding out that we are the Word, the Body of Christ, iconic in the wagon wheel.

It was out of communion with Black friends that I first heard that expression—*Black lives matter*—and as I heard it, it lifted up my heart and mind. I had long been moved by the beautiful fullness of African-American bodily expression through singing and dancing in the hope of what the world might become, and here it was again, coming out in three profound words. This unique dance—a gift of belonging and nurturing—means the world and changes the world. To dare to say "the Word" is to approach the throne of God, and, as St. Francis would say, know that we are "one family." As we open our eyes, we see that sacred place of residing everywhere. We hear it in the Psalms and in the purity of heart and the sadness of sin, the longing to turn the page of our lives and our history.

A number of decades ago, people were writing about the "age of anxiety," a topic that continues to be considered today. We still find ourselves in this age. Have you perhaps found in yourself a certain self-consciousness as social justice or racism is discussed in our day? If you and I are being disturbed, would we turn to the Word, not so much for answers but for the dynamic of peaceful engagement? Tragedy can be a terrible gift if we receive it well, if we allow ourselves to be drawn to Lectio together—the reading of the Word in the world as we now find it. The Word as we seek it is always generative, never death-dealing, though it helps us face that which is dead within us. Would we risk letting it open us, even in painful ways, in order to help us find new life for ourselves and with others?

So, we are blinded and sometimes deafened (totally contrary to Lectio), as our anxieties grip us and we doubt the power of the Word. Our ability to be around or stand with people who find themselves broken or anxious is abandoned when we are not seeing or hearing. The Word in Jesus Christ rose up, within an oppressed group living in a poor town. Mary and Joseph partnered with the cosmic God to usher in the Word. To dare to hear the Word rising from the fringes of society and of suffering peoples, I believe, is to approach "the throne of God."

Active listening is the interactive map of Lectio. We hear and then speak, which is to say the Word is read or proclaimed and then, after some quiet, a conversation begins. All of this, we remember, began in the interest of the Word. It comes to abide in us and give us the spirit of *metanoia*—our hearts healed to renew the face of the earth.

Nothing stops with the Cross if you read it. Everything, rather, *crosses* over and is transformed. We often learn most from those who are suffering, reflecting back to us the ache of the Christ on the Cross. The Cross is something that people of color perhaps understand more than anyone else in America because of how they have suffered. We are all invited to actively listen to a pain or collective ache rising in our midst, which is transformed in us as we are opened. We—our bodies, our minds, and our spirits—are to rest enough to become attentive to the will in the Word. This is why we have poets in our midst to help us see the Real and taste the aches of being human—so that we might participate in Bonaventure's notion of justice: to come to our full stature and return to our original beauty. And, when invited into the transformation of all the world and the new creation that is expressed in the first creation, maybe we, too, reply with the affirmative, "Word, man word."

BE HERE, BE HOME

With the rich gift of living at Mt. Irenaeus is the treasure of solitude. This is a place to become ever more alert to life, uncluttered and uncrowded, as it presents itself to us in the Allegheny Hills. This is where we let the "signs of the times" speak to us, let them read themselves to us, as we might sit back and listen to their voices rising off the pages of creation. Creatures have their own word for us, fashioned as vestiges of the Word. They become, and already are, our Lectio partners. We read with them best in silence and solitude. This all opens out and spills like melting snow and spring rain here in this thirsty, cold world waiting for the Word. As has been mentioned, it was Bonaventure who said that there are two "Scriptures": the first being the sacred text of Creation and the second being the sacred texts of the Bible.

All of this is to be read.

You and I are invited to be lifelong readers.

I have always enjoyed nature but began to read it in a whole new way when I first came to Mt. Irenaeus. When the former owners, Al and Marg Ernst, moved to Nevada, I moved to the small home on the property—a one-story, two-bedroom place that was once a summer home for the Ernsts. We friars gathered there for a while, and it was great fun. Then, within our first year, we added two more bedrooms and two more bathrooms to the back of the house because we had so many people joining us for retreats. We were literally pouring out of the house. At times there might be eight to fourteen students finding spots to sleep at night and two friars sharing one of the bedrooms together.

Our first summer posed some questions. Where would I sleep when the house was filled? How would I deepen an experience of solitude and silence when the Mountain was becoming more active? The full-house experience was its own joy in a wonderfully gregarious place, but I still wanted to commit myself to solitude whenever I could.

So, we bought a tent that would become my summer dwelling. It would be the primary place for sleeping, but also for rest and the chance for some solitude and journaling that I enjoyed. Br. Joe, one of the four friars at the Mountain, had his own tent, as well.

For however full the day seemed—with clearing trails and guiding guests, as well as cooking and sharing supper in the evening hours and completing our time with prayer—walking to our tents at the end of the day ushered silence and mystery.

Sometimes I would turn off my flashlight on the way to my tent at night and feel the grass moving in the breeze that staggered out of the forest above, promising a cool evening's sleep. The tent, where our chapel is now located, sat beneath young maples but also overlooked a valley of rolling hills, allowing me to see the glory of the season and the particular day each morning. The character of our tents could be described as gentle and spacious.

In my tent, I could usually see stars through the netting as well as the speckled glow of the fireflies. Listening in the dark, I found myself thinking about how birds, insects, and animals were in my vicinity, or, rather, I was in theirs. Each had its own relationship with its Maker. I was blessed to be taken into the intimacy of theirs. I was there, unbidden yet grateful for all of this—each one of them alive and in the *conversatio.*

On Carl Jung's doorway was a quote: *Vocatus Atque non Vocatus, Deus Aderit,* "called or not called, God is present." Those nights in my tent, the creatures around me spoke this so loudly in their silencing and going to sleep. What is at the "heart of life" is revealed in the "after hours" experiences—when we stay awake waiting in night's dark mystery. Do we let vulnerability open our senses, or does our fear instead send us searching desperately for distraction? For anybody who has "been there" they know that what I say is true, that God can seem closer in a quiet, dark night.

It's a bit like the way in which a Scripture passage might open. At one point, in the light, it is clear; then it becomes unclear; and then in its own darkness a certain obscurity and opaqueness disappears. We come to understand the Word, often without words. It is an action of Word—uncreated, coming forth from the Father, in the Spirit, through the Word. This allows us a special sense of privilege and does not always have us put the headlights on for our insights.

St. Bonaventure, in his *Soul's Journey into God,* makes it clear that to read (Lectio) and hear is to find our family and the obedience in nature among the creatures in creation. The Latin word *obēdīre,* which means "to listen," was used to describe a Roman soldier who would put his ear to the ground to listen; to discern what is coming. This is Lectio: putting our ear to the Word to sense what might be in the world that needs us to listen as well and letting God put God's ear to our hearts. All is God's Word for us to hear. We are taking our time to place our ear beside creation and the activity of the cosmos, and "we are pilgrims and strangers no more."[57]

We are not strangers in a strange land. Is this heaven? No, not quite. It is western New York, the hills of Tennessee, the coast of California—it is God's home. It is our earth within and beside and among all creatures. I suspect that the good Earth, under my tent and holding it up, simply said to me during those peaceful and frightful hours, "Be here, be at home." Can you hear those five words rising up for you as the day opens, unfolds, and closes?

"WELCOME, BE AT HOME"

I remember when we first started looking to establish a Franciscan community in the hills around western New York or northern Pennsylvania. I had felt the call for a long time, but perhaps like most people who feel a certain pull to do something "different" with their lives, sometimes doubted that call and wondered if I was crazy. How have you experienced this same confusion and perhaps loneliness in your own life?

I suppose this call that I felt stretched all the way back to my childhood. My parents told me that after being in the hospital for eight weeks with a serious illness, I longed to be outside as much as possible. There was nothing I loved more than being outdoors. (I'm in a chair, on a hillside, looking out over a valley, as I review this passage.)

After three or four years since we first made our proposal to start a Franciscan community in the hills, I became discouraged. We had noted in our mission that we didn't want to take land away from farming families, as some nearby developments had done. We had a few serious opportunities during those years, but none had worked out. I was beginning to wonder if we were in over our heads.

One July afternoon, I received a letter from Al Ernst, who had heard about people in the area who had an interest in finding a place for prayer and retreat. I opened the letter, interested in the land he was selling, then saw the price and felt downhearted once again, knowing that we had so little to spend. So, I put the letter aside.

I went on vacation with my family, and it wasn't until I returned that I decided to contact Al. We agreed to meet. I remember driving toward St. Bonaventure University and exiting the highway toward Friendship, New York. I thought to myself, *Oh, that's a good sign.* When I arrived at the property, Al approached me with a stern face and said, "Riley, I was about to give up on you. Let's look at the place." I felt reprimanded and forgiven all at once, and off we went.

Arriving at a series of dirt roads—the last one up the hill that we now call the Mountain—we parked and I walked by myself toward the road that enters into the land at the mouth of Roberts Road on which this farm stands. It is the highest part of the county. The goldenrod and New England asters were beginning to blossom. There was a buzz in the air as bees collected honey from the goldenrod and other wild perennials whose names I was yet to know. I was dizzy with the beauty of it all, feeling like I could almost lose my balance. *This is it,* I thought to myself. It was as if everything was crying out, "Welcome, be at home."

That was almost forty years ago. Just the other day, I found myself walking up to that same spot. It was around the same time of year. It was hot, and insects seemed to be singing and humming. Goldenrod sat off the old road, as well as a variety of other blossoming, late-summer wild perennials. It felt to me like the whole earth was singing. There was an aliveness that welcomed me in. It was as if I could hear those familiar words, "Welcome, be at home," once again. I was once again dazzled, off balance again. So, I stood for a while, quiet, unable to even think of words of gratitude, though that was what I was feeling and sensing.

The whole cosmos is unfolding throughout the seasons, and that day the whole cosmos was singing through each little plant around me, each goldenrod nodding, each Queen Ann's Lace seemingly facing me and somehow saying, in its own voice, "Hello, welcome." Lectio is a practice of coming home, again and again, wherever it is we are on our journeys. Scripture and Creation call to us, welcoming us back—welcoming us back home.

Even if I was leaving behind a group of people whom I loved at the retreat house, I felt the enthusiasm each night as I climbed the hill to my tent. There, I was in the midst of another kind of family: the multidimensional reality of these creatures and all that was in the space, in darkness and in night, in the quiet of the last beam at dusk, and in the hum of the woods quieting.

Remember, this is western New York, with some of the most unpredictable weather in the country. One evening of a very rainy summer, I remember leaving our house and slogging through the thick mud to the tent, wondering, *Why am I doing this?* We didn't have any retreatants staying at the house, so I had a bed and a place to stay indoors. However, I could not resist the call to be out in my tent in the woods.

Throughout the summer, though, I realized what it was that kept me coming back. *The rain.* The more I listened, the more I learned. It was like an album where each song connected with me differently each time I listened—the many voices, the layers of sound, the quiet pauses, the rapidity of the drops, their shapes, and the change in temperatures and conditions that informed their diversity. Often within minutes, there would be a change of voice of the rain. To sit there with my eyes closed and read the felt sense of presence—the movement of water or rain through the area—was a particular pleasure and honor. Especially when I was sitting dry in my tent! Thomas Merton's beautiful essay "Rain and the Rhinoceros" comes to mind here, when he writes about the "festival of rain" and its compelling rhythms in the woods: "Nobody started it, nobody is going to stop it. It will talk as long as it wants, this rain. As long as it talks I am going to listen."[58]

Our first two falls, autumn really showed herself to me. The beauty of the woods became very familiar. I was often there by myself for several days, getting to know the land and the Mountain itself. I felt like they welcomed me into their family. There were old lumber trails (about ten miles' worth, we'd later calculate), through and around parts of our land, which had grown over. Over the years, we began to clear the brush.

The way the light came upon both the leaves of the trees and ferns was especially beautiful in autumn. A few times I was chased by hawks, realizing later that I was probably coming too close to their nests. On those dry autumn evenings, the burnt sienna and the okra reminded me of the Southwestern desert, the remaining yellows and brilliant orange and reds especially against October blue skies. This natural canopy held the glory of each plant that works so hard to bring us summer and is now about to rest, beginning its return to the earth.

The earth is pregnant with the Word. And so is the sky. One night when walking down from the chapel after evening Mass, we turned around and looked westward to see a display unfolding of color and light—the Northern Lights! For a number of us, it seemed we saw a seraph and a cross—sacred images in our Franciscan and Christian tradition. Being before all of this, which is to say in its midst, and taking time to be with it, is what it means to greet the cosmos and at the same time begin to read the cosmos. It is what it means to do Lectio in depth and in breadth with the sun, the moon, and stars.

LECTIO IN THE STORM

We are in a storm, treacherous and challenging, and we need to read our charts and maps. We need to read the face of the sea, as well as the faces of one another. These are the "pages" before us. As the winds shift and the sea changes, we remain in the midst of needing to read this moment and all that is in it. We need the peace and presence of one another to find our way into the holy. As Christians, we find the rich wonder for us is that we have a God who is both one who leads us there and also walks with us on this journey that would otherwise be dark. The one who is the "way, the truth, and the life"[59] and, therefore, *is* the very chart, maps our passage in the face of treacherous storms. We need to find one another on the ship. We find that each other's wisdom will always open the way—and this will be a way of wonder.

I wonder what it was like when the Desert Fathers and Mothers left Egypt in the early centuries of Christianity, searching for a place to be free from an oppressive culture. I wonder what it was like as they gathered in the desert to find solitude with one another in the nourishment of the Scriptures. The desert—what a place to be free! "Systems"—their creators and leaders—masquerade and disguise themselves so that we might almost get lost in their selfishness.

Once on sabbatical, during a very dark time in my life, a mantra arose that followed me while I was in the mountains of California and back to my ministry at St. Bonaventure University, becoming part of my walking the paths there: "Trust, Christ, the walk."[60] It came back time and again, bringing light to my dark heart—in the chambers there that seemed void of anything that sounded like God's Word. As with our sisters and brothers of the time in the desert, and on our streets of America and the deserts of our day, we can pause and risk trusting the Cosmic Christ, the walk of our life. Christ is cosmic because we are in the cosmos and the cosmos is within us, finding its own way today. Reading meaning in life and finding wisdom has great utility, but it is not valued, even in a utilitarian society.

The Desert Fathers and Mothers were reading the storms they had to endure in Egypt, the landscape that lay before them, their very lives, as well as God in the midst of it all. When you are out at sea, there is no turning back. Lectio moves us deeper into life, further onto the waters, where we might discover the courage to live another day.

LECTIO AND THE SENSUOUS

With books come words. With words come cultures and stories and ideas. And within all of that is the way words are formed: their roots found in other languages, perhaps formed in ancient times among ancient people, unsuspecting of the importance that their very alphabet formation might have on our formation today. I find it especially interesting for us, as we open ourselves more and more to the practice of Lectio, to fully immerse ourselves in the text—beyond the words on the paper and enter, as we might, into the *culture* of the people who first shaped some of these words. We find alphabets and symbols, offering us a very early figure of a very natural world, such as "W" for "water" or "wave" and so on.

Some time ago I headed West in a faithful Outback my friend, Les, provided me. The car was loaded with boxes of books and painting material. This was a sabbatical journey. Books have always been a love of mine. Books have been wonderful "to have and to hold" on my lap and in my consciousness as I go about my day. I sense that they bear life. One of my books I had in the car as I headed west was *The Spell of the Sensuous* by David Abram, a book that had opened much within me that year. In preparation for my places to stay and people to see along the way, I called a few authors, teachers, and practitioners. One of them was David, who lived somewhere near friends of mine in Santa Fe, New Mexico.

"Could I see you while I am visiting friends in Santa Fe? And, if I take you out to supper, would you be willing to talk with me about your book and implications I find within it?"

Along with my awe of language and fascination with words, I was interested in David particularly because he is understood to be an eco-philosopher and phenomenologist. He is interested in how things are by their manifestation of being—their action and activity; the present wonder within the reality that we all share the same "household" with one another. In some real way I found in David's writing someone who lamented our rejection of that activity in a culture that is so self-absorbed. Whereas St. Clare encourages us to "sit before the mirror of eternity," in our culture we often sit before a mirror and hardly see anything other than ourselves.

David's vast perspective of our world's story also intrigued me—the joint culture he described between both creatures and the evolution of humans in creation, eventually arriving on this land as people finding our own languages. His emphasis on the sounds of nature, whether birds or seasons, was quite striking in his book.[61] Again, let us not forget that our Franciscan school of wisdom, of learning particularly, as St. Bonaventure notes, highlights the wonder of our senses that they are apertures to the sacred—to the holy, to the Creator. Though I do not believe David considered himself religious at that time, there was a striking overlap between David's work and Lectio.

In Lectio, we invite wonder to rise up in our senses; that even includes the uncertainty that comes with new personal discoveries in the text or our own personal stories. We let the text pull us deeper both into the story and into the moment—sounds that seem to abound in any Lectio encounter: the play of the wind and the rain, or the alert of an alarm or a bird call or an insect moving into their mating season. All are nature's outcries. This is wonderfully driven by the erotic—a longing to be one, in love with another, physically joined with the universe as "stardust," as we say about ourselves.

So, over supper with David at a Mexican restaurant in Santa Fe, we spoke of birdcalls and the wonder of communication between animals from which we learned our own sounds and ways of shaping words and communication. We discussed how humans picked up on a sense of direction—the movement of a possible storm or places where there might be a stream or nearby sources of food—based on Creation's communication with them. In the sounds (we could say "language") of other animals were the ingredients our ancestors shaped into words. They weren't actually words as we now know them, but certainly meaning was being passed. That meaning was written on walls and hides and vellum and pages, spoken and sung, chanted and proclaimed. These were more than ideas. They were actions and names.

That evening with David we talked at length about Moses and the burning bush. Fortunately, our table was a bit secluded, saving others from the outpouring of great excitement and energy as we both retold—back and forth—the Exodus encounter: the invitation of the burning bush to Moses, his response, and their rapport. David was so excited as we got lost in this story together that he almost spit out his pasta salad. That's the energy of Lectio.

David, with his Jewish roots, helped remind me that the name of God given to Moses allowed Moses to tell his people who God was in conversation. *Ruach*, as has been mentioned, means "breath" in Hebrew and suggests the very origin of words. We were fired up as we "chewed upon" the simple dialogue in that story. In all of this, David was breathing the name of God across the supper table to me.

We begin Lectio not first by reading, but by breathing. By choosing an activity that moves us toward stillness rather than being overly agitated in anticipation of what might come to us. It is not passive, but active openness. Again, learned and having its own habits, Lectio is unbridled again. We are reclaiming the practices of ancient ancestors. Like riding wild horses across the plains, we are opened to the sounds of creation as we find our direction in the foundations of each of our languages. Even when our time suggests its own darkness, it is nonetheless birthed in the light of the Christ of the cosmos. The practice of Lectio is not so much about the expendability but the extendability. The plains stretch out before us—if we dare get on the horse and ride it.

"YOU DO NOT OWN US"

I came upon a clearing one mid-October day that I had not visited since early summer. Now the grass was tall, glowing with a warm yellow, like an extra-large portion of butter melting on your favorite toast. The plants stood there, seemingly full of life before winter, though they had all of the felt sense of the end of its season. I was completely taken by their beauty, standing tall and gracious, with flowers now dried and looking more like feathers, fragile blossoms untouched.

I thought that I had walked up the hill into the woods alone. I thought I was there in this backwoods by myself. But standing with the goldenrod, beguiling me by the marvel of its beauty, I heard something that was "as clear as the day"! The goldenrod simply said to my admiring heart and wide-open eyes, "We are free, and you do not own us!"

I don't remember if I took a step back. Nor do I remember if my mouth fell open, but I know my heart and mind opened all the more. (That is what this book is about, isn't it?) Only the earth was with me to witness this experience. It seemed this plant spoke for the rest of the goldenrod and the trees and the earth. Then, it said it again.

"We are free, and you do not own us."

Having made its statement clear with confidence, it was quiet again, and I was as well. One could begin to critically evaluate this moment psychologically, but the words remain and the moment gives us all a wonderful message. Somehow, someway, I was spoken to. It was a very real message truer than anything else I could have thought about that day.

In our modern world we seem to objectify just about everything, claiming what we "own" to be "things." We are borderline obsessed with capturing and containing, rather than acknowledging first their vitality. We had done a great deal to establish the Mountain in trust, with this goal in mind, so that it would be held that way and not be treated as property or a commodity. If Lectio is about the living God speaking, everything God has created has a voice. If you and I believe in the Christ who has set us free, everything that is living has been set free, and is going to tell us that in one way or another if we take the time to listen.

For me there was contagion in the goldenrod's proclamation. It caught fire in my heart and spread again into my understanding of other aspects of, not only the land we call the Mountain, but other aspects of life that can feel overly ego-identified or prized property. The goldenrod showed me they are none of these. Rather, they are truly "members of one family," as St. Francis would say. They are companions on the journey.

If that last sentence is mere poetic expression for you, pause. We are listening to the whole of everything, as it is articulated in each living thing. The liveliness of the activity of plants, trees, and the cosmos is to let us know something about the God who is expressed in them, a God who was humble enough to become the Word, breathing in and through them to us, here, now. There is a contagion here that is a proclamation of the Good News of Jesus Christ calling us to be free. How is the Word rising from these *different* members of our *one* family in your own life today?

Lectio can happen, I know, deep within me when I bear the awareness of God's Word and allow the voice of God to arise through almost anything and everything. Each creature, whether or not it is formed in a way in which I find appealing, has a voice, even if scratchy or distorted.

Proclamation isn't always pretty. We see this especially in Jesus Christ, who became bloody unto death. But the Good News *is* beautiful, and so are we. The loudness of our goodness and the glory of God shines through all of our woundedness. I'm reminded of the great Chinook prayer: "May all I say and all I think, be in harmony with thee, God within me, God beyond me, Maker of the trees."

I write this after rereading the first draft of this book. I am acutely aware that my words cannot hold "the water of all this meaning."

The sound of the wind is now coming like a train through the woods around me, and the trees are more than just "clapping hands," as Isaiah would say.[62] My hermitage is solid, thank God, built on rocks, in fact on layers of shale, and not on sand. At least the structure of my life is stable, as I seek grounding in God's Word and presence. I'm humbled by this setting I'm in today but sobered by what is still broken and unsettled within me and in our world.

The Word really is here, not patting me on the head and telling me this is a lovely place, but, as with each of us, inviting growth from the ground up, even from between rocks and sand.

A tree cracks a few times, and a very large branch falls as the wind whips through, coming and going in different directions, leaving me wondering whether the branch made it all the way to the ground. Our lives are sometimes this way. My mind wants to see what fell, but I'm going to stay on the porch.

I notice my windows on my car are open and go out to close them, making sure that my items inside are protected from the rain. I climb back into a semi-protected screen porch to enjoy this storm as it surrounds the Mountain. Protected, cozy, and accompanied by the storm, I find myself thinking of the brokenness of our nation and world, as well as the rising up of three profound illnesses: the pandemic, which is reaching far and wide; our inability to language our illness and relationship with the rest of creation and lack of desire to foster relationships beyond utilitarianism, knowing that pumping more oil doesn't help us anymore; and the reality of racial inequality, reaching all the way back to the wonderful, innocent people who were brought here in enslavement. The latter weighs especially heavy this afternoon. Even when we thought we were helping through days of integration and anti-segregation, we never faced the full pain and suffering of persons and families of enslaved bodies. The trauma lingers in minds, souls, social relationships, and people's capacity to live fuller lives in America. All of this is dark, I know, probably darker than the storm that rages around me.

My father is also on my mind this morning. He has recently "reappeared" in my life. I suspect often those who died suddenly seem to return to us occasionally. I'm not speaking of them as ghosts, though some may experience them that way. I'm speaking of the beauty and power of their person unleashed in mysterious ways—in colors and comfort, in wordless conversation, in wisdom that has seemingly come to me straight from his heart to mine. We have no ownership of moments like the one I'm in or the one you are in right now. They are *sui generis*: "one of a kind." These moments are their very own and not able to be owned.

As I reflect upon my father, I can hear my mother's words: "Your father would have been a great coach," she told us longingly after he passed away. He was. He is.

The light is almost green in the trees around me now. The hills here are drenched in rain that is falling so densely I can barely see some of the trees. The pond below me is a blur. The leaf—my friend who found me over five decades ago in the woods in New Jersey—has long gone home to the earth and to its Creator. In its own way, it rises today beside my father in my memory and helps me remember that we truly discover our unity in these simple events. It rains here now, containing the woods and feeding them. More leaves will become dear friends.

Lectio is our capacity to see and enter into the beautiful. As Lectio would lead us, we must let ourselves know that we are not observers—we are *participants*. That is the radical call of Moses's engagement with Yahweh through the burning bush. Presence invites participation. The covenant today is participating *with* Yahweh and *in* other people's lives.

I look out at the perennials here in my hermit's garden, down toward the pond, and feel memories of gardening with my father. I'm reminded of shaping flowers for our altar at the New Jersey novitiate, as I grieved Dad's passing. Early Franciscans encourage us to be sealed in the cross of Christ in places like this—where we are drawn aside to read our lives again, to look back on earlier pages as we look ahead, and feel and find images and signs of God's writing. We heal our wounds through the wounds of Christ. We all encounter death. Yet it all rises and can be seen near and upon us. Perhaps tired and uncertain on our own path, we find this "nearness" again as clouds break open and light comes in on us. I find myself thinking of the path through the novitiate woods that opened out into a clear field on that day that the leaf found me. The sunlight was there for me in the field, and that same sun was in the leaf. My father was taken home by the Spirit to be with the Son in the Father.

I read the colors around me on this day. Blue has always been my favorite color, and I believe it was my mother's, but I never asked my father his favorite color. I remember the day he brought home a "new" used station wagon—all green! It became, as my dad was sometimes, a great attraction for all the children in the neighborhood, as they climbed in and around this shiny used car, totally fascinated by its collapsible third seat—perfect for carrying his five kids and his wife. My dad was happy, proud, and delighted in the joy everybody displayed that day. As I sit here in the rain, I look over and realize that the car I drive is the same: a Subaru Outback (a wagon!) and as green as my dad's.

In Lectio, some things trail on. Trails open and pull us over, drawing us further through new narrow city driveways and out into large landscapes. We read along the way—not always what's on the page, but on a person, in a face, in the day we are living through, the path we are on, the memory that rises, the rain that falls upon us. It is less about what we find and more about being found.

PART III

CONTEMPLATE

TRANSFORMATION
THROUGH THE WORD

"Contemplate . . . you will possess mansions in heaven with him among the splendors of the saints and your name will be recorded in the book of life."
—ST. CLARE OF ASSISI

"Let us always make a home and a dwelling place there for him who is the Lord God Almighty, Father, Son, and Holy Spirit."
—FRANCIS OF ASSISI

"The deepest level of communication is not communication, but communion. It is wordless. It is beyond words. It is beyond speech. It is beyond concept. Not that we discover a new unity, but we discover an old unity. My dear brothers and sisters, we are already one. But we imagine we are not. And what we have to recover is our original unity. What we have to be, is what we are."
—THOMAS MERTON,
Informal talk delivered at Calcutta, October 1968

everal years ago, I was walking with a childhood friend of mine, Margee, on a hiking path beside Genesee River Gorge in Rochester, New York. It was a special place to both of us. As children, we played in those woods, climbed all over the paths, and even wandered around the edge of a waterfall that plunged forty feet down into the lower part of the gorge. The trees were close to us. And it was as if the waterfalls were a gift to us. I remember always coming home from the woods feeling like I had a secret, the very goodness of the world.

That day walking with Margee, decades removed from our childhoods, we had followed the path down by the ponds and were now making our way up a paved path where there had once been railroad tracks, back in the 1950s. As we walked along the path, we appreciated the space to talk about deaths of loved ones and reminisce about our childhoods. The background became foreground as I listened. I began to hear more and more the voices in the woods—a breeze in the trees but also the familiar sounds of a brook and a waterfall. I could hear the brook's voice, and I knew it was still there, still speaking. This was—in so many ways—the same voice that I hadn't heard for over fifty years. I turned to Margee, struck by the beauty of the moment and the place in our friendship, and asked her if I could take some time by myself. I asked her if she would mind if I ventured further from the trail.[63] Margee smiled and

said, "Of course," and into the woods I went, hoping to find an old trail that I might remember and rediscover the water's voice.

I clawed through what felt like a hundred bushes and eventually found myself in a field of New England asters and goldenrod. I began walking through the woods and eventually crossed over to a path along the gorge, a trail I remembered well. Then I was off through the woods toward the falls. The water's voice was even more clear and more familiar. Eventually, I found myself standing on the edge of the bank above and beside the falls, taking in—and being taken in—by the small waterfall that my friends and I had known so well, so long ago, as "Brown Falls," a place of wonder and marvel for us children.

Here I was, a child again.

But this was not a moment of nostalgia. It was a moment when time fell away, when childlike wonder sent me searching, there toward this fountain of water. Margee and I had both had full lives, but that same voice we knew so well was still talking. I knew this voice, and I had been graced to hear it again.

A voice that spoke to us in those early days was now calling out to me again as fresh and clear as a stream. Of course, other things had altered our little waterfall, but quite surprisingly, a large stone had held the eroding earth back, allowing the water to continue to cascade below. The falls were pretty much as I remembered them, filled with mysteries and stories. There was even a little indentation up on the hill on the cliffside behind the waterfall where we used to crawl behind the water, feeling we had found a cave. It was a place to crouch and look into each other's very young faces and realize we were in our own world, at least for a little while. This "cave" was especially helpful in strong, rainy weather when we would find shelter. That space was still there and in some ways beckoned to me once more.

I stood there for a while, looking up at the maple, ash, and birch trees, probably progeny of my friends from childhood. I turned from there and, not putting those little falls aside, I took its spirit with me, which it freely gave me again. I had accepted the invitation to go further. To go further is the great call, risk, and freedom of Lectio Divina. It is the "next step"; it is finding permission; it is finding the teacher and listening to her voice.

Leaving the page is not what Margee and I were doing that day. We were *taking* the page—the whole book, all of Scripture, indeed a microcosm of the cosmic, the whole book of our lives, an ancient path—with us, into the world and finding it there, realizing it was with us as God had promised it would be with us. All of this was both a "homecoming" and a sending forth; the finding of an ancient path at a new time, thus discovering a new path.

As St. Francis of Assisi tells us, "Create within yourself a place where God might dwell." I believe if you are reading this you have already created that place in some way and have prepared a site where God can dwell within you. Maybe today it burns brightly as a bush or as gently as a candle, but it is always there, opening our senses and letting our hearts come alive, so that you and I might not only see that all things are being made new but also might take part in the becoming of all things—and all people becoming new. I'll close this section's introduction with these words from St. Romuald, which you might considering using in your Lectio practice today or this week:

Sit in your cell as in paradise. Put the whole world behind you and forget it. Watch your thoughts like a good fisherman watches for fish. The path you must follow is in the Psalms, never leave it. . . . And, if your mind wanders as you read, do not give up; hurry back and apply your mind to the words once more. Realize above all that you are in God's presence and stand there with the attitude of one who stands before the Emperor. Empty yourself completely and sit waiting, content with the Grace of God, like a chick who takes nothing, eats nothing, but what his mother gives him.

THE ARCHITECTURE OF LECTIO DIVINA:
The Dwelling Place of God and God's Choice to Dwell Among Us

Lectio begins when we create a place within ourselves for an encounter. The Crucifix and the mystery of Christ's dying and rising are an architectural structure for this. Yes, it is a construct of a horrendous and despicable event, but it is not the event itself that is the architecture. God's love made this not as a punishment but fashioned it as mercy for us as we move into the fullness of our being in the Christ of the cross. What is often called the Paschal mystery—the passion, death, and resurrection of Jesus Christ—is also the architecture of the changing seasons and the nature of the cosmos. The primary meaning of Christ and of all of Christianity, therefore, is visually and physically present and here for us to read in the Crucifix.

You might remember that St. Francis and St. Clare both gazed upon the San Damiano Cross in prayer and in this sense did Lectio with the Crucifix. Let's return to this theme here as it spirals out for us, as contemplation transforms our hearts. The Crucifix and the mystery of Christ dying and rising is a *mysterium*. It is all here for us—to *listen*, to *trust*, and to *follow*, a trilogy of words I received in prayer many years ago. As we continue to read the Word together, what is the movement you sense? Francis found throughout his life that in dark passages came an incredible brightness: how the mystery of the Crucifix *leads* us, *lends* to us, and *allows* us to see clear through the dying and rising of Jesus into the love that comes forth from the One who is eternal, the One who bore his Son for us into the world through Mary.

The Incarnation is God's ultimate conversation with us. In our coming to hear the story of Christ's death through sacred Scriptures and now standing before its artistic portrayal, the Crucifix, we are invited not to re-create this within ourselves, as if to inflict upon ourselves unnecessary suffering, but to know that this is what the Created One did for us. There is no quid pro quo here with the Cross. Our human transactional ways have tried to transport us into an explanation of "Christ dying for our sins." Instead, we must move into a wonder, as we are invited to love totally and completely— to give ourselves away. This is a love and a life that transforms sinfulness.

Love poured out in Christ has informed, fulfilled, and renewed us and the face of the earth. This is the core of Franciscan joy. Joy does not cause us to look away from agony, pain, suffering, and certainly not the Crucifix. We do not come to the Crucifix, as some might say, as if to fill up at a "spiritual gas station." Rather, we read the reality of this and look deeply into this mystery. We "walk in the footsteps of Jesus Christ," as St. Francis once said. Before the Crucifix, we are called again to walk deeply in the human journey.

There is no bargaining with God, even when our prayers sound transactional. We sometimes pray like children, and that's a beautiful way in which we pray. We might pray something like, "God, if you do this, then I will do that." This misrepresents the God who freely gives God's self and knows our every need; who, even in our dark passage of contemplation, comforts us with the deeper knowledge of this intimate awareness. But we should also acknowledge the fact that some of us shy away from speaking "theologically." Each of us speaks of meaning in our own unique way.

In Franciscan Lectio, we paradoxically remember that words are frail carriers of meaning. They are not meaning itself. This encourages a tolerance of certain ways of speaking and an acceptance of others' appreciation and their own expression. Some of us come closer to a more scientific way of speaking, whether academic or rational. But the study of theology, spirituality, and mysticism has always been most sound when it came from the *sensus fidelium*—the great Latin phrase for the sense of the faithful; those who are walking, living, and talking in their daily lives. Pedestrian folks who carry on a vernacular theological experience are much like Francis of Assisi who discovered meaning by being among others and creation.[64] In a world where we tend to define one another by our ideas, may we not let words become a "stumbling block" to extending compassion to others, nor to ourselves. Perhaps we might even sense the Word rising up in the heart and life of one who speaks quite differently from us; or maybe in a situation in which we feel self-conscious in our stammering or rambling.

May we again trust "the school of love"—a phrase monks have called their living in a monastery—without feeling that we have to arrive at a monastic theology (which, don't get me wrong, is still a wonderful gift to the church and world). St. Francis gives himself a theological pass, less sophisticated in his expressions than Clare, possibly because she was "better educated." Yet both of them reclaimed old images, metaphors, expressions, and felt senses of being in the world that were particularly significant for their time and, indeed, were in some ways revolutionary. They can be a special gift for us today if we "taste and see" what they meant. Through their own Lectio lifestyles, they remind us we are all sacred, "fearfully and wonderfully made" as the Psalm says, from the hand of the same Creator and in Christ's own image.

The sheer joy and hope—the well of love—that Clare and Francis see in the Crucifix is a contrast to other holy men and women, particularly of their time. The cross was sometimes seen as a sign of judgment and sin and suffering (and is still seen that way today by many). This notion clouds and confuses John's understanding of God, which is outpouring love and self-sacrifice for humankind and all creation. This radical giving forth of self that is ours and God in Jesus Christ is more than just astounding; it asks us to slowly read and, as if beginning to read again, "sound out" every consonant and vowel of love. The cross for Clare and Francis has us turn out toward a suffering world rather than turn in and berate ourselves over our own sins.

Without a roof to cover their heads on the road, early Franciscans *uncovered* their souls and spirits in reading the Word. It remains a great promise, in particular for those who have yet to hear it. This is the very motivation of Francis. He invites us to "go among the Saracens and others who do not believe, and, when it pleases God, preach the Good News." This sense of missioning, which is not to live *over* in a controlling or ruling or proselytizing sense, but to "go among"—to live *with*—echoes and reflects the very movement of

Jesus himself who came among us, not to take us over or take us away, but to lift us up into the wonderful mystery of God's love for us. Lectio begins with the comfort and ease of space, like a simple house, and then becomes spacious, like a mansion, with a place for everyone at the table. It reaches beyond the place we are in and develops a sense of God's dwelling place in each of us and all of us.

MEASUREMENTS AND THE UNKNOWN

Maybe you love woods and streams as much as I do. Or maybe they are not your familiar eco-zones. You might consider when and how you might enter them! Follow a nearby trail or path that you have never been on before. Allow yourself to wander without obsessing over the time or a particular destination.

On one sabbatical, I was leaving a friend's house in Taos, New Mexico, and driving through desert land. Back then, cars were up to date if they had a cassette player built into them. Mine did. I was living the dream! I had been following my map as I drove through the desert but decided to pull off onto an unfamiliar road and trust its direction. The Vermont monks were singing from the cassette, *"Journeys ended, journeys begun, To go where we have never been, to be beyond our past."*

I can still feel the freedom and the childlike delight of entering onto those "unknown" roads. The contrast between the Southwest— the hills and mountains that rise up out of the desert—and the North- east—my appreciation of woods and streams—was invigorating for me. The beauty and expansiveness of both are significant, but they manifest wonderfully in different ways. Here was open, vast, and seemingly arid country, yet I knew it was alive.

To explore the world wherever we are is a great gift we've received. It need not be a long journey or a dramatic quest, but it is important that we allow ourselves to *journey*—to know that we are pilgrims and that our bodies, souls, and particularly our hearts have the ability to stretch and find their way through darkness.

I do not remember who first wrote that "everything is a burning bush," but this statement is an invitation to experience wonder while we are wandering. Our capacity to find what we need is often through letting go, as we "take nothing for our journey." The full and dramatic theophany of Moses is now ours—to take a path and then have the courage to step off that path, even if there is a domestic or corporate reason to stay on. Gerald May, a great contemporary teacher and counselor, found experience was often his best teacher. There is good humor both in retelling encounters and also in experiencing them. That is what humor is—the unexpected coming upon us! In the known and unknown, the holy wind is our guide, often shaking all of our branches and scattering every leaf.

Think of it! Throughout history, billions of creatures, humans included, have tried to find their way, whether while listening to a song, the call of another bird, or a baby's cry. The smell of anxiety or peace. The change of a river's course and the angle of the sun. People prepared a fire to let others know where they were. From Robert Bellah to Bill Plotkin to David Abrams and others, these authors let us know that relationship existed from the beginning of creation and animated evolution.

Our human journey is beyond the usual metrics and their fine tools. And so, Lectio Divina, and the Franciscan style in particular, helps us to be gently rattled out of our usual way of calculating. There is a usefulness to measuring, but objectification wrings beauty out of life. Lectio can feel disturbing at first, but it is not destructive. It wakes us to a world that is more colorful and creative, more communicative than we ever thought—not only as an object to be observed or "measured" but something cosmic to be in conversation with. This is part of our Franciscan understanding of ourselves; we truly are itinerants and "mendicants of meaning." It's for us to consider that we are beggars on the journey, alongside others and their longings, so that we all might come to be a bit more deeply and purposely in the service of others in creation.

Lectio is a type of wandering with Sister Wisdom into the unknown. It is a true on-the-road experience that is not only happening in our room where we sit, or in our chapel, or as we drive, but as we go anywhere and allow ourselves to be led off the path, into that which is unpredictable.

A GOOD CAMP IS NEVER FINISHED

When we were kids we called them "the woods." Those trees ran along the Genesee, which we called "the river." Then there were "the fields," spaces to play and be ourselves at the bottom or our street, which was a tightly packed little working-class neighborhood in Rochester, New York. Our homes were pleasant and wonderful under the shade of large elm trees. The woods and the river and the fields, we felt, were ours to explore.

The backyard was its own place of care—a place of mystery and wonder, where my mother tended her garden. We learn wonder in small and large places, and it helps us to transition to the immensity of the world and the wonder of "the garden" everywhere.

On warm summer days, parents would let the neighborhood kids wander freely. We children were our own cartographers. We made maps. We found our way. We dreamt of where we were going and went there. We would think about where else we would go—to the fields, down to the woods, around the trees, over streams, down trails. We were explorers without having named ourselves.

The big question when summer began was always what we would build during summer break. Would we try to build something of a tree fort? Or maybe dig a ditch with different rooms? Would we shovel out an underground hideout, like in the war movies, or an aboveground cluster of teepees in a field? It seemed we always longed to build some kind of temporary encampment.

The word "ecology" comes from the root *ecos*, meaning "home" or "household." *Logia* means "study of." So ecology is the study of different homes and the members of households. Ecology requires that we de-Americanize our approach: we're not just looking at the structure of the building, or the property value, or private ownership—we are looking at the members of the household. During those summers in my childhood, my friends and I were learning by feeling our way through the fields—that simple understanding of what was growing there and feeling that we were part of it.

I will always remember one of the most spontaneous and motivating wisdom sayings offered up by my friend David Peer. We had just broken off a stand of small sumac trees and had piled them up. We assembled teepees with leaves on top to create canopies where we could crouch and feel like we had a temporary home for hiding. As we sat inside these little structures, as if to test the homes we had built, we shared a candy bar.

Dave climbed out of a teepee after taking one bite of the candy bar. He inspected our teepee, made sure it was upright, then turned toward us with a sweaty red face and, with a big grin, said:

"You know, Billy, a good camp is never finished!"

The glee of this child's saying has remained with me. Sometimes we go to places that seemingly do not have meaning, yet we still find ourselves finding a pole in the middle, the axle, that which organizes a small camp. One pole can do it all.

A good camp is never finished.

Maybe that is part of the reason why our one-line mission statement at Mt. Irenaeus is "to join with Jesus Christ to make all things new." Revelation, in this sense, has so much to say to us. What would it be like if we all began to "make all things new"?

Dave was part of a revealing moment for me. It's a moment that continues to call me, encourage me, and invite me to risk. I can still feel and smell our "camp"—the sound of insects under a hot, late June sun, the unique aroma of sumac after it is cut and laid down in a hot summer wind, the crushed grass and snapped twigs under our feet. It is its own soup. It is a wonderful smell. It is an aroma for our ears, eyes, and nose to drink in. This is the wonderful mixed-ness of our inner and outer senses that I believe Bonaventure reflects on in his own language system. He crowns this singularity of creatures in their glory with this descriptive phrase *haecceitas;* "this-ness." His understanding is that if we come to know God and have an ongoing willingness to receive the Revealed One in creation, which he calls "the first book," we will have greater access to opening sacred Scriptures. There will be more doors and lintels, more gateways to God in the book we call the Bible.

What are you stirred by that would have you explore the world around you or in you? What to you is a good camp? What would it look like to risk working on the camp again?

We come alive as we explore. We find maps, *logia*, or *loci* (which means places, spots or locations) inside us. An intuition perhaps arises. Maps reflect a desire to see and know direction—to journey. Our inner senses connect with who we are as we enter and spend time in Lectio. We are held by life as we hold the Word of Life. "Camp," or *campos* in early Italian, is the same word for "field," which leads us back to Lax's notion of rising and coming into the field. Out of the darkness of our night, we rise to discover light on the face of all things, for we always know we are at home in the camp. In us, Christ has established his own camp—a camp that is never finished as we are continually transformed in contemplation.

WORN TRAILS AND RHYTHMS

When walking in the woods, I sometimes stop and become attentive, realizing the Word of God is right before my eyes to be read all the time. The earth we walk on is ready to awaken. If we are deepening all our senses in Lectio, we are becoming more alert to the earth's capacity to "speak to us."

Feeling the weight of our institutions in what we call the postmodern world, we might be full of wonder as we meet God's simple, gentle presence in the pre-modern world of the woods— the postmodern world meeting the pre-modern world in God's presence! Maybe the trails through the woods are familiar. Maybe the walk around your neighborhood is the same route it has been for ten years. Maybe the Gospel passage or the letter from Paul or the wisdom of a prophet or the emotion of a Psalm is familiar. Maybe you know it "like the back of our hand." Though Lectio has an aspect of familiarity, it is not predictable. Lectio opens us to rhythms of wonder; to the radical course of our lives, even the trials that could have taken us under.

The *radix*—the root—in the forest of Lectio is the Tree of Life (Bonaventure's metaphoric icon for Christ) that holds us together, from which we bloom like the root of Jesse. Metaphors cross over and multiply each other in this forest: the Word, the Light, streams of Living Water, All In All. This is the *mens* that St. Bonaventure writes about—the guts, the core, the heart, the liver. Over time, and in different ages, our spiritual teachers have noted from what organ this inherent power originates within us, from which place is the deposit site of a person's consciousness and being and where the Creator is noted to reside. The Hebrews used to think the liver or stomach was the center organ. It took a while to realize the "heart" was central. We hear this centrality reflected in Francis ("Create within yourself a place where God might dwell") and St. Romauld ("Empty yourself and sit waiting, content with the Grace of God").

This is the depth to which we are to be transformed by the Word! Old habits and rhythms are replaced by new ones. This is also an aspect of contemplation. It is both as simple and as complex as that. Some of the discovery that may bring us into Lectio as a habit is that all people have stories. They are for us to hear, and Lectio is how we hear them. Often, to follow the trail or rhythm of any of this is to arrive in the clearing of God's own campfire.

One Thanksgiving weekend, I decided to venture off the path and take a walk in the dense stand of trees and shrubs. As I climbed, the trees turned, and at one point, I came to a place where they were so thick that I had to fight my way through. They had, at a much earlier time, been planted as a Christmas tree farm, but these overgrown Christmas trees were never cut. Within twenty minutes or so, I had worked up a real sweat and some anxiety, feeling that I did not know where I was.

As I kept muscling through for several minutes, I came to where the trees turned up the hill and was almost *flung* out onto a path—a path I was sure I had climbed before, some other season, some other day, perhaps years before. I felt there would be a coming shift in my awareness, but at the moment of breaking through the darkness of the trees, into the light of the path, I had no idea of where I was. My surroundings teased me with a sense of knowing. It was startling that I was so disoriented, and at once it was a tantalizing experience.

Old passages and sacred Scripture can be like worn trails. Lectio Divina can be a practice of falling out of familiarity and finding yourself in the dense, dark quiet of a place on the path that is just a yard or two away from home base. Coming home is such a blessing of Lectio. To quote T. S. Eliot again, "We shall not cease from exploration, and the end of all our exploring will be to arrive where we started and know the place for the first time." That line in his poem has landed in my soul often in my life. It opens my heart to the ongoing activity of discovery that the God of the living is indeed a living God.

Babies, apparently up to a certain number of months, have not yet discriminated between their own body and their mother's body—between the bottle, the breast, and some other object in the room, indeed the room itself. Everything *is* baby and *for* baby. Early discoveries of individuality are significant moments in a child's life. These are sacred moments—to share in gentle delight and discovery with one another and then, from there, life's long journey as we grow and return to "the mirror of eternity," as St. Clare calls God's own presence and image.

We are always clay, but not putty. We are not to be pushed around. Rather, we are held in the hands of the One who chooses us and has formed us. Let's return to St. Irenaeus's words:

> *It is not you who shapes God*
> *It is God who shapes you.*
> *If, then, you are the work of God,*
> *Await at the hand of the artist*
> *Who does all things in due season.*
> *Offer him your heart, soft and tractable,*
> *To keep the form in which the artist*
> *Has shaped you.*
> *Let your clay be moist lest you grow*
> *Hard and lose the imprint of God's*
> *Fingers.*

St. Irenaeus, who is full of beauty and metaphor in his commentaries, allegorically points the finger again toward mystery, asking us to look more, not only even at the moon, which is lovely, but at the sun! We stand in daylight. This again is the larger sense of the intricate reading of the moment that we are in, our being alert to the small places and pieces of life. We might say this is the "cosmology of the everyday."

When children come before a mirror, it is always a particular treasure for parents. "Look how beautiful you are!" a good parent might say. Eventually a child will realize that others, too, are different and have their own individuality. As we begin to see another as "the other," even today, might we remember what our loved ones said about us and mirror this affection toward the "stranger"? Might we dare see the good in others and hold what is around us with esteem and affection? Some of us (and maybe all of us to some degree) have lost touch with this "original unity," as Thomas Merton called it. We are, each in our way, seeking to regain this deep, rich second naïveté: the ability to see how wonderful and one we are, having each journeyed through times of separateness and pain.

We are servants to one another—gates, windows, and doorways to richer knowing and coming to know. We are the wellsprings of experience, the Body of Christ. John's Gospel—that book Francis loved so much—helps us hear that richness over and over again. John found his poverty in the flowering in the belief of superfluidity— that overflowing fountain fullness that St. Bonaventure would later call "God." We might say that John's Gospel is mystical. Everyday mystics are not always mountaintop people; they are breaking bread and living daily lives. Yet they see life without borders, even while understanding life as ordered. We walk streets and pray a word as we smell exhaust—all with others, all at once. *Lectio, meditatio, contemplatio, oratio,* and *actio*—gaze, consider, contemplate, and imitate—all weave in and out of one another throughout our days. We have the capacity to swing open the gate of the garden we've never visited and walk there, whether the garden is under our feet or in our imagination. To go beyond the limits of the page is an important part of Lectio Divina, for everything is a door, a gate, and a window.

DOING THEOLOGY FROM WHERE YOU ARE

Key to Franciscan Lectio is its *locus theologicus*—the site or place of the divine encounter and how the intimacy or meaning of the experience might impact our world. In other words, it's *doing* theology—coming to some understanding of God—from where you are. Let us say it again: it is doing theology. As Pope Francis wrote in his encyclical *Laudato si'* ("On Care for our Common Home"):

> Francis helps us to see that an integral ecology calls for openness to categories which transcend the language of mathematics and biology, and take us to the heart of what it is to be human. Just as happens when we fall in love with someone, whenever he would gaze at the sun, the moon or the smallest of animals, he burst into song, drawing all other creatures into his praise.

Our "early theologians" did not restrict theology by possessing or positioning it. Their theology happened in conversation—in the communal opening of the Word and preaching at Eucharistic celebrations. In refining doctrines—as they were still coming to some clarity and often with some significant conflict—fruitful theology happened in conversation. This added layers of meaning for all the people who were present, their senses, and more! It called for listening.

In this context a type of *kerygma*—a "proclamation" of the faith— unfolded. This faith seeks understanding and is ongoing. This is why we call our lives "graced." Our Creator is revealed in the Christ, and Jesus walks beside us and resides within us, as St. Francis tells us. We are able to become involved with a Lectio practice that sharpens our eyes, opens our ears, alerts our hearts and all our senses to what we will never be able to contain, but "what holds us and fills us to the brim," as St. Clare wrote to Agnes of Prague.

So, an early understanding of theology does not "place it" in a pulpit, lectern, or desk, as its *locus* (place). If there is a "place" for theology, it is in the heart of encounter, the place of our everyday life. We might think of it moving from solitude, where we encounter dark mystery, to *conversatio* and silence, through contemplation to action. In action is our transformation. Theology unfolds in the heart of the one who believes and is seeking to believe. Or, we might say, theology is the church as it seeks to believe together and manifest this faith, which is a gift to us all and calls upon all our gifts to manifest in the world today. Theology informs our seeing, thus our living, thus our willingness to suffer and even die for one another.

This leads nicely to a Franciscan *locus*, which is anywhere we have come forth from God and will return to God in Christ. In other words, anywhere in the cosmos. St. Irenaeus talks about how we quite literally bump into God or some of God's "vestiges" in the world. Our God has left marks, signs, and wonders in each creature. St. Bonaventure speaks similarly of "vestiges." The place, then, of theology and faith is coming further into the fullness and blossoming interactivity of the divine and our world. This can be anywhere, as

Merton famously points to, even at the corner of 4th and Walnut in downtown Louisville where Merton "was suddenly overwhelmed with the realization that I loved all those people, that they were mine and I theirs, that we could not be alien to one another even though we were total strangers." Christian mystics and Franciscans believe God rises up in many places, but that does not mean we believe in many gods.

Once when I was in Louisville, Paul Pearson, director of the Thomas Merton Center at Bellarmine University, let me out of his car near the corner of 4th and Walnut (which is now called Muhammad Ali). Sporting a sophisticated smile, he said to me, "Go have your own epiphany." I was very self-conscious after he said that. I had longed to visit this famed spot because of the beauty of Merton's mystical experience there, but that was *Merton's* spot. He had drunk that well dry. How could I have my own epiphany?

As I walked toward the corner, I saw five adults or so, possibly homeless, sheltered in the entrance of a closed store. One of them was a woman. I looked at them but then felt I should "turn away." I was on a mission, after all. Oblivious to Merton's experience—that he had seen people in the city walking around, "shining like the sun"—and feeling self-conscious because Paul's car was still running in a no-parking zone, I continued toward the famed corner.

I walked a few more steps and noticed that a woman who had been in the group had followed me. The woman stepped closer as we arrived at the corner of Merton's mystical experience. She asked if I might give her something. My journal now tells me that I "turned toward" her. I told her I only "had a dollar," as I had left my wallet in Paul's car. I gave it to her, embarrassed it was only a token, and wished that she could find a place for a cup of coffee or soup.

We both stood there with noontime people passing all around us. I continued, "I am Dan. Could I offer you a prayer or blessing? Would you offer to say one for me?"

She said, "My name is Anita, and I can't read or write."

Somehow I blurted out, "Anita, I believe you can pray from your heart."

She began to speak a prayer with words and then a tune in the midst of the crowd, beginning to sing them with great freedom and delight in her eyes.

We drew very little attention from people passing us who were probably focused on other thoughts or things. I had almost missed her as well, concerned about getting back to Paul, and on to lunch so that we might talk about Thomas Merton and his writings. I smile now at this many years later. I almost missed Anita on the very same corner where Merton said, "I have no program for this seeing. It is only given. But the gate of heaven is everywhere."

Franciscans are not the only ones who have this disposition, but followers of Francis and Clare certainly see themselves in the midst of the wonder and glory of all creation. They see themselves beholding beauty as they meet other creatures one at a time. The place, site, or *locus* from which one does theology, then, is the *relationship*—not the idea of it. We would say that this is the dynamic of Franciscan Lectio: a spirit-filled journey that we make through our life in the Word. We are always immersed, as if baptized again in the "fountain fullness" of the triune God—in the vestiges of sacraments through everyday encounters. I wonder where Anita is today.

"THE HEART OF UNDERSTANDING"

In the late 1990s, I made a retreat with Thich Nhat Hanh and his monks and nuns, as well as over 300 other people—adults and children of different traditions and diverse backgrounds. With all of us gathered in a large but simple assembly hall the first night, his presence welcomed a silence that fell upon the room. But he did not quiet us as much as he enlivened us by reverently looking at us, as we did Thay. Thay was seated, and, after some silence, he looked up, smiled, and said: "You have arrived, you are at home."

These very plain words and his great reverence for us made a place in our hearts and invited us to be open to his teachings. I was struck by how uncomplicated, clear, and fresh his insights were, unsophisticated in his phraseology. He opened for us rich, deep wisdom and practice that reminded me of our father Francis and some of St. John's writings.

In our retreats at the Mountain over the years, I have found myself wanting to share Thay's simple greeting. Looking out into a group, I often sense nervousness. People are likely wondering what is next, who all the people are, and possibly even where the toilets are located. I find that silence—an initial few moments of quiet—helps us with all our questions. As stillness is welcomed into our midst, I love to quote Thich Nhat Hanh and simply say something like:

"You have arrived, you are at home."

"The Reign of God is at hand."

Or, as Luke suggests in his wonderful Gospel, "The Kingdom of God is within you," or, "Come, it is already now."

This deep sense of "home" is already in us. It was so striking for St. Francis that he repeated it regularly, as did St. Romauld, as something that we "prepare within ourselves" so that God (Father, Son, and Holy Spirit) might dwell. This is the abiding Word of God, always triune, that has found its way into us. We have arrived in this moment. And in this awareness, we open a way for the Word to make its home *in* us, into our hearts, and into all of who we are. Arriving does not imply that we have come to a stoppage in time or life's activity or responsibilities, but rather that there is something of the moment that is full and rich and complete, that the Word is alive and active here. Especially for Americans, or, as they say, "type A" persons who are always "on the go," it takes conscious work to taste our arrival, to sense that we are already at home. There is something in us that almost resists this feeling that something has been accomplished outside our will. We all need to find relief from the hyperactivity, heightened responsibility, and restlessness of our age. I'm again reminded of the great Gospel story that tells us "it is already here"—the banquet is set; the kingdom of God is at hand.

Rich hospitality flows from someone who is "at home," which is to say a person is at home in themselves. This arrival to a sense of at-home-ness is a contemplative journey. Like Francis, we are invited with Christ to "repair" or "rebuild" within ourselves and the world that "which has fallen sadly into ruin." We are hearing early on of a God who "stayed for dinner," who eventually filled the upper room and our homes and hearts with daily bread and everlasting life.

God is welcoming us in, serving us, first washing our feet before we are sent forth to do likewise. One who is experiencing the habit of growing Lectio Divina in their lives "reads" God's signature everywhere and in all things. Bonaventure, as has been mentioned, called them vestiges. We might also call them fossils—God's very life and activity as God chooses to stay with us. God, we might say, is embedded in the earth and within our bodies to set us free.

We are at home. Thich Nhat Hanh called us to a place of peace and abiding—a place that is ours in a world that is always on the move. That is the call of Lectio: to come to stasis, to a certain stoppage, to a place of solitude and peace. This stillness, where we stop trying to control everything around us, can feel like "letting go" and is indeed somewhat of a "little death," opening us out into a further fullness of life unfolding. This is the passage that invites to come to a sense of unity rather than division. It is a movement to a radical sense of *welcome*; it tells us that we have arrived, that there is nothing disparate, that all is one.

Again, Blessed John Duns Scotus's understanding of "this-ness"[65] is a particularly rich insight into the simple oneness of each person while, at the same time, acknowledges that, though there is no duplication or multiplicity of any being, there is profound and rich relationship of all beings, all creatures, and all individuals with one another through their very creation, and their Creator. This is more than just a link, but is rather the flow in activity of who we are through Christ as we hear in Colossians 1:15–20, a passage so rich it is always new.[66]

Sometimes in our interactions with others we think to ourselves, "Who do they think they are?" But of course we are not who we think we are! In fact the beauty of our distinct difference and goodness flows from our very being and our ability to retrieve that experience with each other. It has us sit with our unique individuality rather than be defined by our differences. This rich particularity of a person, of an idea, of any creature, is something we should want to be able to read. This "reading" is a primary activity of daily life and is conjoined in our activity of Lectio so that they flow one to the other, both as a learned practice and as a faith stance in the world.

INSIDE-OUT PERCEPTION

When we are able to see reality in a more cosmic, spherical, circular or spiral way, as Teilhard de Chardin and now others would suggest, we begin to feel the encompassing of that which is at the heart of us.[67] At the very core of who we are is Merton's 4th-and-Walnut reference—"the person that each one is in God's eyes."[68] The "firstborn of all creation" dwells within our hearts. This is amazing to even think of, isn't it? Let alone hold it quietly in our very being and mull it over? The Creator of heaven and earth abides within us and is somehow enthroned in "tents" within each creature and person.[69] This is more than animation. This is not a shy God who hides out in places. This is the humble One who fills the world and, as the Psalms help us see, experience heaven and earth resounding within the One.

The point here is to come to a deeper sense of, not precision, but order: what is formed, what is shaped, and how it comes to be in the world around us and in some sort of order within us. We might even wonder, "Who orders ordering?" It's easy to see how we think it is the role, even the purpose, of humans to keep things in order. In fact, many of our systems reward us for our managing of time and business. That is not to put those things aside as unimportant. Indeed, they are. But the point here is to come to a deeper sense of what is precision, what is formed, what is shaped, and how it comes to be in the world around us and in some sort of order within us. Have you ever thought of cosmic ordering with this kind of perspective? If we think it is up to us as humans, or even "believers," to maintain order, we might find ourselves reacting to anything unfamiliar.

There is grace, and grace is active. As it is active, it manifests itself in the activity of others, as grace is the gift of God's life to us in our midst. It helps us to be operatives—active and engaged—not functionaries, and certainly not robots. Rather, in some rich, divine way, we are collaborators, we are co-operatives, we are co-members with Christ in making all things new.

Many of us grew up with an outside-in preoccupation about goodness, wellness, and success. Goals for each one of these were often placed before us in objective light. They were put up on chalkboards. They were written in books. They were lectured to us, in no uncertain terms: how to do things right, how to be right, and how to succeed. These outside-in directives were meant to help us climb higher in the world.

Wellness and holiness may look different from the world's portrayal of success. Lectio enhances the possibility of these times of conversion. We don't always think of prayer as processes these days, but Lectio can very well be a process. It's ironic that we would take time *off* to find a way in which we would take time *on*! But, as we take on the rest of our day, we move with a more consciously ordered interior. This, in the best sense of the word, truly "radicalizes" what we are doing.

An outside-in way of perceiving—this "ordering order" as it were—has us responsible for retaining, and quite literally policing the world at times, continuing to determine and fight each other by what order means. With Lectio Divina and other practices, I believe our biggest discovery, over and over, is *metanoia*, the change of heart that sees things as they emerge from the heart of God and from our hearts.

I consider Lectio an organic model of ordering. As we understand the purpose and position of Lectio, I hope by now we sense that it is more about presence than about perfected practice. Lectio, again, is not a project or practice that asks for completion. Our clocks have moved from reading the sun's position in the sky to setting alarms on our phones. We can be held "prisoner" without knowing it. Lectio, really, is about radical gospel liberation—the reason why our desert forebears journeyed away from the city into the nothingness. They were actually fleeing the confines of culture. They realized there was something else, something more. This radicalization of the journey is what Lectio is.

Lectio invites us to look at life and everything in the face; to see the present moment as a gift and not judge it. Indeed, the Word itself is bringing all things into order, drawing them into the unity and community that is God, the ongoing and eternal dynamic that is, as Acts says, "the one in whom we live and move and have our being." Lectio moves us from the Western world's preoccupation with how things should be—a moral and legal ordering—to visit the place where life rises up as an expression of the beautiful.

As the Mountain began, it seemed to find its identity in the example of Francis and Clare. We sought to "find some rule," which is to say a habit or way of living in a disordered time as disordered people seeking that deeper sense of order. Francis and Clare saw divine love and covenant as that which organizes more richly and fairly than top-down, outside-in social structures. A person's worth comes from within and is not formed by what they are "without" by the world's standards. The Trinity is a dynamic way of understanding or alluding to a God that is, at all times, forever moving. But not frenetically. Not out of anxiety for order. But rather because order *is*

God's self. Like a large wheel or mandala, divine order includes and encompasses all. Most cultures have intuited a mandala and often crossbeams through it that we would, as Christians, recognize as a possible sign of the cross. This is the very place in which we kneel before the "throne of grace." This is God's heart in the darkness of the coming together of life, not yet first conceived as order, but first found as life ordering order.

Order is cosmic. Order is expansive. God reveals the simplicity of an all-present Creator. Artists have always reached toward balance, union and communion, harmony—the beauty of life even in what seems first to be grotesque. From within, our God emerges. We experience something that is not over our heads, but up from our hearts and hands—all the power "to make all things new."

SENTINELS

The archetype of the sentinel is one that reflects many great saints. Though sentinels in the Psalms and Isaiah are not the same as the ones we call the prophets, they have a similar responsibility in that they alert people to God's presence and coming promises. As Isaiah 21:67 says, "This is what the Lord says to me: 'Go, post a lookout and have him report what he sees. When he sees chariots with teams of horses, riders on donkeys or riders on camels, let him be alert, fully alert.'"

Sentinels are a security system for people gathered in a village or camp. They are noted in the Scriptures as being up on the wall at times, alert to anyone who might be approaching. The sentinel, in both Hebrew experience and literature, is a type of mystic who has a very practical and necessary position for the people of God. When the village people were gathered with their families for the night, vulnerable and asleep, sentinels were the watchmen on the wall, always on guard. Sentinels, in the ancient world, were ones waiting for the dawn—waiting for the sun of justice to arise—alerting their people of the enemy traveling in the darkness of the night. One might say that sentinels held a somewhat lonely position, but an important one.

Often in prayer or meditation, people will speak of a recommended posture. The archetype of the sentinel inspires us to be alert, as if we're always up on the encampment walls; to be attentive and aware. Like the sentinel, we ought not fear solitude. We are sentinels, alert to both God and the possible coming of an enemy. In our case, that "enemy," so to speak, might be our attachments, illusions, egoic projections, or sin patterns. As we serve as sentinels, our senses are alive and alert. We anticipate with hope rather than fear. We long and cry out for God rather than crouch and worry about threats. Over time, if we find this as a helpful pattern for meditation or contemplation, our four Lectio movements might be *waiting, watching,* and *wondering* as we prepare to do the *work.*

Lectio Divina has a quality of rest about it—a peaceful resting that is not a nap, but is a felt sense of being protected and cared for. Those who lead it, as well as those who gather for it, are in one way or another the agents of that safety. We become sentinels even in our hearing of the Word—in our waiting, watching, and wondering— even before we work or live our day. It is all service. This restful attentiveness of the sentinel is analogous to a participant in Lectio. We settle in to become more alert—to let our "inner eye" open so that we might be attentive to all that we might see from our *heart,* the very eye of our heart. This is authentic seeing.

A little movement or a change in the setting . . . a simple shift in our horizon . . . the sight and smell of another . . . an unexpected sound . . . All of these things arise in prayer and alert us to be carefully aware of all that is taking place. Our bodies are natural systems of knowing. Our own senses are our sentinels.

PART IV
IMITATE

TAKING THE WORD INTO THE WORLD

"Were you there when the morning moved over the grasses? Were you there when the sun looked through dark bars of clouds at the men who slept by the cookhouse fire? . . . Have you looked at spheres of dew on spears of grass? Have you watched the light of a star through a world of dew? . . . We have known these things from the beginning of the morning, for we woke early. We rose and came into the field."
—ROBERT LAX, *"Circus of the Sun"*

"Every day is a god, each day is a god, and holiness holds forth in time. I worship each god, I praise each day splintered down, splintered down and wrapped in time like a husk, a husk of many colors spreading at dawn fast over the mountains split."
—ANNIE DILLARD[70]

"I pray not only for them, but also for those who will believe in me through their word, so that they may all be one, as you, Father, are in me and I in you, that they also may be in us, that the world may believe that you sent me. And I have given them the glory you gave me, so that they may be one, as we are one, I in them and you in me, that they may be brought to perfection as one, that the world may know that you sent me, and that you loved them even as you loved me."
—JOHN 17:20-23
(read to Francis at the time of his death)

*A*s I write and rewrite, and as Stephen and I edit this book again and again, I realize, once more, that we are up to our ears and eyes in a treasure trove of "light, happiness and peace." This simple phrase was placed by the church in the preface for the Eucharist on the feast of "Christ the King of the universe, the King of the Cosmos." Christ is the great Word of God being light—the activity of God's "light shining on matter," as we say with art and artists. We can only hint at all that is here for us as we fall more and more in love with the Cosmos and its Creator. Francis's Canticle of the Creatures takes us deeply into this intimacy and vastness. So much of what is new (all of it, in fact), is rooted in our past, our personal and communal histories and the history of Creation. Which brings us back to the wheel.

The wheel—discovered over 3000 years ago—has been essential for so many other "machines." The potter's wheel. The spinning wheel. Even the washer and dryer in your home. The invention of the wheel improved our earliest practices. Pottery developed further with nuanced strength. Weaving became more efficient and intricate. We ride on wheels. We rely on wheels for turning on our water or closing a window or opening a door. That circular movement of gears . . . or a simple tire . . . or even a wooden wheel . . . are all foundational today. Wheels are essential to human life. They have developed over time and taken on new expressions. The wheel has never been labeled "out of date."

Then there is the spiritual side of the wheel: mandalas; the great circles in our religious traditions; the kivas in the southwestern desert, where people would gather as equals for their common conversations in a large circle built into the ground, indeed grounded in conversation (*conversatio*). You might also remember that a large, old, handmade wagon wheel has guided our spiritual movement at Mt. Irenaeus.

I've again found my heart returning to that old wagon wheel while writing this book. I'm awed by its history, its legacy. How it likely transported crops around the time of the Civil War. How it may have carried runaway slaves to safety. How it may have carried locals down the road to listen to Frederick Douglass preach. That old wagon wheel was vital as our ancestors moved about this land, and it continues to move us today into new spaces.

Wheels help us *move*. As Clare's quadrants lead us to *imitate*, and as the quadrants that rose up out of the Desert lead us to *actio*, we are reminded that core to Lectio is serving those in the mystical body of Christ who are suffering. What do Francis and Clare show us in the care of everyone, particularly the care of "the least of these," those who are the most vulnerable? Their understanding of beauty and the conversions of the outpouring of God's love is something that they are able to read on the face of the poor and the simple. Rather than being frightened off by what they see, they experience an invitation, a call to come near, a willingness to extend the fullness of oneself to someone whose face and very being is the map of God's presence. As Francis did with the leper, he decides that he wants to go *toward*, deeper into God's presence, not away.

Another practical way to frame Lectio is *remembering, reflecting,* and *responding*, which I believe mirrors Clare's quadrants. By graced insight, Lectio would move us back into our usual occupations and relationships, but possibly into new ways of engaging others, responding to their needs. "Respond" is a small word with a large responsibility. In Lectio, there is a taking responsibility for what we've heard and what has been given to us. Responsibility *is* responsiveness to others. We see in it the authenticity of Christian prayer, for all prayer needs to be as Christ was: ready to pour oneself out for the love of the other. Prayer does not remain as adoration or gratitude but moves in some way or another to considered action. The purpose of sitting down and reading is to get up and live. But we respond because God responds to us. First God made us, created us, and set us here—and now God invites us to participate proactively in ongoing creation.

The ancient name for Christ, *axis mundi*, the axle of the world, is such a beautiful image because it helps us see the three-dimensional reality of ourselves and everything else. It is moving. It has the ability to move, to carry others, to lift and carry, to do essential work, to attend to the needs of the land and to other people. Because, to see this wheel and its image in the maps of our cosmos, the core and axle begin to rise up in our hearts as contributing to an unseeable scene: Christ the Lord. The Word of God opens us up to this. It shows us that it truly is the gift of life itself. Lectio is a way of reading life, sitting with the Word and being quiet. Indeed, we were doing Lectio on this wagon wheel when we found it over thirty years ago, and we are still learning more and more about Christ, the "Axle of the Cosmos," the Axle of the world, the pole of the tent, the heart of the Love that has a compass. For that book there are no chapters, and its table of contents is self-evident to us all as we do Lectio. We practice being cosmic.

When I was a child, most movies were in black and white. The double features—often with cartoons—were the real draw for going to the Saturday movies, especially when one of the movies was in Technicolor. But as you know, the movie experience has changed and indeed expanded, having gone through its own metamorphosis.

Next they added trailers, or, what they called "coming attractions" after "newsreels," which we still had in the fifties. I remember when the curtain was pulled back to the usual size for the trailers, and then, in an almost historic moment, pulled back further . . . and further! The width of the "silver screen" seemed to stretch halfway across the world, from "sea to shining sea!"

Cinemascope, Panavision, and finally Miramax pushed what seemed to be the natural limits of not only the width of a movie screen but the arrangement of the theatre—how films were made and what we came to expect of them. Producers and directors sought to take advantage of this incredibly beautiful width made available— at least in part—by new lenses. The theater, as a visual experience, was reconfigured for us in its scope to contain even more, inviting us to look into a vibrant world.

Physicists tell us that reality stretches and seems to reconfigure as it is presented or revealed to us in our lifetime. We might say that it morphs. It truly changes in form and depth, in shapes and sizes. With this lens, there is great excitement and the chance for new perceptions of what we call reality. Curtains will pull back further. Revelation is ongoing.

You can almost begin to feel why I talk about this in relationship to Lectio, which can remain two-dimensional and monochromatic, tightly contained on a Bible page, and opened and closed when one wishes; or it can be pulled back further. You and I, in this book, are reflecting on this revolutionary reality of the Word of God, which does not break open, but is indeed beyond all dimensionality and takes us beyond definitions and plots and storylines, even though all of these are great benefits. You can feel the axle again—that moving and spinning reality. And again and again, we can sing and dance. Love *does* have a compass.

We gather with and around the Tree of Life, not only as a cinematographic portraiture, with all our senses alive. Our livening senses no longer allow us, it seems, to be only "observers." Lectio, like life, is not only going to the movies. Our Creator is inviting us to see all that is around us with expanded vision—product perceptions, greater receptivity, and availability to what is going on before us—indeed, what is happening now.

Our spiritual imaginations are ignited—or maybe better said, the spirit of hope and love within our imagining the world: the gift to imagine all that can be returned to its original beauty. The virtue of hope is meant to emerge as a virtue of the heart—that we "hope in what we don't see," as St. Paul says.[71] As we move toward, or as it seems as if the expanding screen is moving toward us, we are invited to form and shape our own experience within it.

Our spiritual imaginations have an ongoing role in our activity of Lectio Divina. Imagination is the wonder and beauty born in imaging. To form and shape images, to receive images, to communicate through images, is both an integrative and generative activity. It offers us an alternative way of seeing (and often hearing), which is to say that we live our lives with more of an awareness of its compelling beauty, perhaps analogous to being engrossed in a movie.

As a Bible sits on my lap, or as a community has a sacred text resting on a desk or a candle on a table, we wait for the curtain to be pulled back further and for the screen to expand. We are invited to awaken our senses and to ignite our spiritual imaginations. The gift to imagine—whether it's redesigning a home or an office, working at a church, taking on a new job that invites us to reinvent ourselves, or allowing our hearts to wander into wonder in Lectio—is one of God's great gifts to us that allows us to be more human.

Lectio, through St. Clare's quadrants, leads us up to this "always, already" God of experience. Lectio offers us up from the text and texture, from the colors and sound and timbre of a voice, from the quiet of a space. All reveal the continuous movement of our Creator in the cosmos, the flow that is the Alpha and the Omega that dazzled many of us, from Irenaeus to Chardin, from Lax to Merton, with Francis and Clare dancing in the middle of all. We stand and sit; we lie in awe; we rise to re-create with God through the dynamic of listening, trusting, and following. In God's ongoing revealing of God's self, like an artist or cinematographer who helps to ignite our slumbering imagination, we might move to what we are viewing, hearing, and reading with expanded senses. In, through, and with Christ, all this is happening beyond measurement. The Word is off the screen, off the page, alive and active in our hearing. It is dynamic, not only in the room of our sharing the Word, but now unleashed again into the world!

Lectio Divina unfolds even as we lift the Bible and sense it in our hands, valuing its shape and size and knowing that as soon as we open the cover, life springs forth anew. This is imagining. And it is the truth in the sense that our imagining helps us awaken to the present depth of the moment—all its potential. It is a "coming to see"—and not just on the mountaintops but even through and within the darkness of our lives, through and within the darkness of unknowing, re-learning, and unlearning. In commenting on the Eucharistic covenant we have, St. Augustine once said, "See who you are. Be who you are." In Lectio, we are invited to see what is not yet seeable because it is our love and faith that has us hoping in what we don't see. This trust forms a unity here and now in the hearts we have—a unity that extends to hold both that which is shattered in darkness and the wholeness of light. Sometimes in our own darkness the Word feels hidden, and our imagining might open our senses to a sliver of light beaming through a crack.

Our ability to imagine is a gift that is given. As St. Matthew says, what has been given as a gift should be given freely.[72] So there is a freedom about imagining that unleashes within us creativity and the constant possibility of living life to new depths, not only thinking new thoughts, and again moving beyond ourselves.

There are so many ways that the religious imagination plays, proves, and expands, so many ways that it shapes and opens us beyond words to the Word. The context helps the text. It does its own work of weaving, drawing us in, helping us to "see with new eyes." The blessed and holy environment, the landscape of Lectio, establishes a ground for faithful imagining. We might remember the phrase "Lights, camera, action!" The light of Christ. The camera of our heart. In Lectio, we hold, take in, and record—*action!*

Hold . . . gaze.

Take in . . . consider and contemplate.

Remember . . . in seeing all of this, we follow and imitate.

Lectio, whatever your chosen pattern, always wants to move toward action!

As I reflect on other insights in this book, I regard them as just that: *sights*. We point the camera and see deep within ourselves and one another the ongoing movement of a world that is taking shape and form because it still is in the Creator's hand. We come to the Living Word to be shaped from the inside and the outside as well. These insights are not meant to become encumbrances, certainly not additional baggage to carry with us into prayer. Rather, they are to be thresholds to the door of prayer that might take us where we will walk freely and further into the home of the One who dwells within us. What do you see as you point the camera?

CODE WITHIN COVENANT

I grew up in a family that prayed together. I learned about Francis from living, breathing friars at St. Bonaventure University. I was graced with awe and intimacy at once. Having discovered a Bible sitting in front of me as a freshman in college, I was initiated into a rich sense of monstrance—vessels that would bear Christ, the living Word, and life itself. I sensed that in front of me was a long love letter to all of us. I hope by now you understand that these personal moments are already yours, somewhere in your life or this very day or waiting to be.

Back before "the book"—before we made books and other conveyances of story—the Israelites' relationship with God unfolded in a series of covenants, coming to its fullness in the blood of the Lamb, Jesus the Christ. St. Irenaeus, one who helped draw together what we call the "Canon of Scripture," spoke not of "Old or New Testaments," but rather of unfolding relationship: Covenants that God made with Noah, Abraham, Moses, David, the Hebrew people, and the Gentiles. In the Christian tradition, Christ is the fulfillment of the Word from its very first expression, both in the cosmos, and in Moses's exchange; in the earlier covenants and before the first Canon. So, we can see why, in Christ, there is "no north, no south, no east, no west." For those of us who humbly stand within this covenant, we will experience (which is to say *understand*) that God in Christ is truly "all in all." This offers us a way of seeing covenant and code.

Irenaeus named each time God "made a covenant" with a person for that person's people, and he showed the lineage of sacred Scriptures through this lens. From this perspective, we begin to see the outpouring flow of a God who has always been in relationship with us—a God who seeks further to mature us, renew us, or begin again a covenant with us. Simply put, the Bible documents God's covenantal story with us . . . by name.

Code (or law) has meaning *within* a covenant expressed. A concern with religion has been that, in trying to get the code right, covenant can seem overshadowed. We have sometimes lost touch with God's "fountain fullness"—a love that has *always* been overflowing; the channels of these Living Waters are never completely ruptured. Ironically, many have felt the sting of judgment more than the balm and promise of redemption. Jesus, at a time when religion had been hijacked by code, walked the earth and said, "Take on my yoke."[73] Returning to Bonaventure's expression of justice ("Justice makes beautiful that which had been deformed"), many of us feel deformed and hide our brokenness, rather than knowing we are already redeemed in Christ, as we hear from St. Paul and St. John. One of Bonaventure's other themes for justice is *rectitude*—a coming to stand upright in the light of God's love. We are God's children now.[74] Jesus helped people return to original beauty—to see the code for what it is, an expression of the covenant, not an iteration of it. Life flows from the One who initiated the covenant with us, the One who is truly righteous, full, and complete—the One who is love.

Prayer and Lectio involve returning to covenant. Our very being returns to tasting and seeing God's goodness and ours. This fills out the *practice* of a code. If you and I are looking at these "spiritual disciplines" merely as activity—perhaps empty tradition or a task to complete—we might miss out on the divine relationship that is now ours in covenant. Our performative focus or idolization of disciplines can be an example of where code and covenant become divorced, at least in our approach. Piety-driven spirituality can feel detached from covenant.

However, we are here together now—under one tent, around one pole—experiencing covenant and code in our world. Does your spirituality animate renewal, balance, and integration? Or do you need covenant to break open code? Lectio is a corrective to all the religious confusion. Lectio doesn't allow us to sit in our own personal spirituality, like a narcissist "praying" by a pond but preoccupied with his own reflection. I might be in my pajamas, but I am in everyone's company when I open the Bible.

A friend of mine who worked with wineries in Sonoma and Napa told me about a wonderful French term, *terroir*, which, in a basic sense, means "of the region." He may, for example, speak of Burgundy, a region where grapes are grown; but *terroir* is an even more intimate particularity: a certain hillside or soil or the effect of the sun or rain upon it. Again, there is an intimacy here, a certain "power of slowing" in the rich meaning of *terroir*. This is more than environment. It is an earth-based word, developing excitement for what is already present. In *terroir* there is a relational dynamic.

Relationship helps us return to the wonder of covenant when we've become preoccupied with code.

Justice and peace and the integrity of creation (now popularly called JPIC) are expressions we hear in the preface for the Feast of Christ the King of the Universe. In other words, a covenant of those core relationships—activities as they are expressed in our lives in *relationship* to our God—becomes this large spherical reality of core presence, and ours with God, that heals the brokenness within the sphere. From within the relationship, we witness the peace of God poured out—this cosmic reality seeking to come to fullness in God. Trusting that there is a covenant reminds us of an invitation that is always there. Our response to covenant is simply this: to fall in love, again and again and again.

Our church history unfortunately reminds us of preoccupation with code—with "spiritual perfection" or our "moral growth." Bernard Haring, one of the great moral theologians behind Vatican II, helped Catholics turn back toward their relational origin. We were never alone in our progress or process. We were never separated from the One who brings all creation to life. This enduring, everlasting relationship that Moses discovered when he asked Yahweh, "Who do I tell my people who you are?" is part of what we re-discover in Lectio Divina.

This psychological and spiritual situating of ourselves is quite a blessing and essential to beginning Lectio.[75] We gather as if in a cosmic kiva. Human, plant, and beast . . . all belong here. None of this is only an activity or idea. It is not just the pursuit of perfection. When we look at Lectio Divina as truly a spiritual art practice, we might awaken to the reality that we are being made, again and again, in God's own image.

As Franciscans, or as those who are inspired by the lives of Francis and Clare and their brothers and sisters, we want to bring (and be brought by) "the Good News" to the marketplace—the very culture, cacophony, and collisions of our world. This calls for practice and discipline; thus, we have the term *disciple*. We are finding our way, learning our way. The gospel is the way of living this out—our very practice. Jesus is our teacher. He stirs our longing to learn, which is our longing to love as a disciple. This is not "up out there" cosmology but is rather "down," as in "in here" cosmology. This is not exteriorizing or distancing as we imagine "cosmic" often to be, but intimate, while at the same time, all-embracing.

As with Francis, this allows us to "go out to all the world" as we are wrapped in one garment of truth and love. As with Clare, this allows us to foster boldness in the face of worldly forces, which, in her context, were the powers of the Pope and Emperor. Each in their own way, Clare and Francis teach us to turn to the Word as we turn out to the world, to find ourselves in the world, then turn back to the Word for wisdom and understanding. Lectio within the cosmos leads us further into the spaciousness and immensity of the *Logos*—one hungry person, one crying baby, one row of cabbages, one Psalm, one chapter of John, one Celebration of the Eucharist at a time.

No wonder the ancients threw their cloaks over their heads whenever they sensed God was addressing them. The power of seeing God is so awesome it would have us "see God" in everyone and everything. There is something that dies in all of us when we "see God." The Buddhists, in another way of talking about this radical conversion, explain it as the death of ego. As Thomas Merton so beautifully wrote in his experience at Fourth and Walnut in downtown Louisville, we would all go about genuflecting before each other everywhere!

This is where Lectio leads us. Perhaps some of us were part of a previous rupture between piety and practice. We are still catching up with ourselves, as our notion of justice, peace, and the integrity of creation keeps expanding with time. We see that the arch in Christ's body is his outpouring service, sacrifice, union, and communion, intercession, and promise, for all creation.

We come to know our God best when we abandon ourselves to God. This nourishes a radical sense of a covenantal God rather than a god driven by code (again, laws that interpret the covenant). Relationships, then, are primary; and rules are of benefit to relationships rather than the other way around. Code flows from covenant. When covenant is forgotten or subservient or second to code, there is an aberrant sense of the human person and a distortion of our relationship with God. Fear grows within our hearts.

If not for Francis, theologians suggest the Reformation might have happened 300–400 years earlier. Francis broke open code and helped people return to covenant. We continue that tradition today.

Early Franciscans took time in the woods, then in villages, then in workplaces and piazzas, calling others to the healing life of God's presence in the world. Not yet an "Order"—a system of delivery— they nonetheless delivered the words "alive and active" in their hearing and in others' hearing. There was something new and fresh in what those early Franciscans were doing. They were demonstrating there was no middleman—no divide between us and God. The Word was immediate and direct in the way the brothers were living. There was, within it, a nascent notion, an early expression of Lectio Divina operative among our first brothers.

Francis and his followers were itinerants as preachers, hermits, and people who worked part-time jobs or begged along the way. It would be interesting to be in the company of the earliest of Francis's brothers and see how profoundly diverse they were, both by way of education and what we call social status. Some of them gave up great houses and land to follow the Poor One of Assisi. Their primary task—their "full-time job," if you will—was to live in community with *each other* and to bring the Good News to *others*. Out of their deep relationships with God and with one another flowed new relationships. New bonds formed that helped shape a new world. It is a movement from the micro to the larger, from an inner life to an outer life, from intimacy to community, and with this the development of a vernacular theology rooted in covenant.

SIDEWALK LECTIO

Early in ministry I found myself leaving meetings and needing to pause. I'm known to be "talkative" and enjoy the company of others, but I am actually only moderately extroverted. Few believe this because of how much I enjoy being around people. But I often sense this call to stop and step aside while in the middle of walking somewhere else. I call it "sidewalk Lectio."

This practice was born on a sabbatical when a mentor of mine, at the conclusion of some very rich sessions, looked across his desk at me and simply said, "Dan, why not *play on your own field?*" I knew exactly what he meant. He was giving me permission to be my true self in Christ. As Thomas Merton writes in *New Seeds of Contemplation*, "For me to be a saint means to be myself. Therefore the problem of sanctity and salvation is in fact the problem of finding out who I am and of discovering my true self." Merton matures the discussion of this question in his lively essay "Learning to Live."

The suggestion that I might want to play on my own field was a wonderfully liberating statement and one of great confirmation. It disposed me toward a style of ministry I was beginning to see in St. Francis's own playfulness, even in the midst of suffering. Each of us stands on our own ground, ready to enter our own game. We come to know there truly is ground under our feet, and it is the ground on which we *should* stand. It's out from there that we joyfully become "players" *in* and *with* the rest of the universe.

In a sense, you are an expert from where you are standing. Have you ever dared trust yourself in such a radical way? You know what is there because *you* are there, reading the Word and the world and the Word in the world.

Francis and his followers became theologians for the marketplace, for the poor, for the lepers, not because they were learned in what we call "book knowledge" but because their faith took them to the first and always essential encounter of Christ in the other. This is why Bernard McGinn, a noted scholar of medieval mysticism, names the Franciscan spiritual movement, as well as mysticism, as *vernacular* theology. It's sometimes difficult to not be lost in our heads about other people, other places, other times, judgments, or comparisons, but Lectio invites us to *read* right here and indeed find our own language. This rich cosmology does not deny the human reality of judgment—it just invites us not to be taking time with it. In Lectio we seek to adopt a pre-judgmental, childlike stance where we are still taking things in or letting others take us in. We see how all our realities are woven together while still maintaining our individuality, our uniqueness, or, our *haecceitas,* as we call it.

Maybe you, too, have found yourself playing in another field much of your life—and perhaps you even do it in a fairly natural way—but don't forget to take time to play on your own field. Time in solitude is one of my great joys. Nature was my primary companion when I was a child and remains my place of great delight. This in no way changes my desire to be in the midst of others, but it does help me trust with comfort my natural disposition.

Henri Nouwen, who had a great gift for taking English phrases and pointing to contrasting meanings within them (even though English was not his first language), denoted a difference between remembering and memorization. Nouwen asked the question, "What do you know by heart?"[76] For a while, people thought that they came to faith by remembering doctrine or memorizing prayers, but Nouwen pushes us further and encourages us to ask the more intimate questions: But do I really know my faith by heart? Has it stirred me to my depths? Do I act fully and completely out of what I've memorized? I can regurgitate things I've memorized, for example, but that wouldn't say anything about whether I've lived my life according to those things. Our heart's journey is about finding freedom from these possessive interior elements to the greater discovery of "who I am."

Sidewalk Lectio started years ago for me. I would be walking somewhere on campus and would feel compelled to become attentive. It was an inner call to silent alertness, to reacquaint myself with what I longed to "know by heart." It was amazing to pause on a sidewalk during the wintertime—to stop the hustle to the next warm building and simply see the glory of the day, to watch the snow fall on various surfaces, to look at a tree or gaze upon a frosted image. This simple pause helped make me available to the Word that is at once so cosmic, vast, everlasting, and here—immediately present, intimate, and fully aware of my every need.

I remember hearing that call again just the other day on St. Bonaventure's campus. On a day when I was lost in ideas, caught up in ego conflicts, wrestling with the results of a meeting, calling into question in my head something that was said at a table, scrutinizing something I said, overall absorbed in the inner noise you may be familiar with, I paused on the path. I breathed. After breathing, I began to walk the path I shared with others. I walked in quiet attentiveness, opening my senses to the gifts plainly given, with signs of life all around me.

When I began this practice, as I stopped on the path to quiet my mind, I would often look around me to see if anybody was watching me. Caught by my own self-consciousness, I might think to myself, *I should probably keep going, I should be on to the next thing.* Sometimes I listened to that fearful voice. Other times I had the awareness to combat this linear lie with truth: *I don't want to get going. Before I get going again, I need to let something move in me that will take me deeper into the depth and beauty of life—not just ideas.* It's interesting, isn't it, how the move toward freedom—which is to say *from* self-consciousness—often moves through a time of consciousness of self until the plane is going fast enough to rise? The air cannot be seen or captured like the ground on which the plane has just departed.

With the flow of students around me on to their classes, I would sometimes feel compelled to move as well, but this time differently: to let my response be a simpler walk, step-by-step, sometimes even naming the steps:

Left, IN,

Right, CHRIST,

Left, IN,

Right, CHRIST,

Left, MERCY,

Right, LORD.

And so on ...

No matter the combination, the two-word mantra seemed to deepen within me. It was my way of letting the Word break in on me. Thich Nhat Hanh's mantra is also a personal favorite: *Peace with every step.*

We take one mindful step after another, opening our hearts to the *actio* of the Word itself. It invites us to no longer close out others or the world because we are too stuck in our heads, attached to our ideas. In these in-between moments of our days, a lot of our thinking takes us nowhere—only deeper into anxiety. In disconnecting from our ideas that weigh upon us, we humbly let go and open ourselves to *really* receive whatever word or phrase has found us: lyrics from a song on the radio that morning, or a phrase from evening prayer, or reading Creation from the sidewalk. Lectio happens, not only during the hour or fifteen minutes of prayer time, but it unfolds whenever our souls are thirsty for the Word that was and *is* being proclaimed. We pause and let our dry hearts become open cisterns waiting for living waters. This interactive *meditatio,* that is, the door to *contemplatio,* moves us deeper into life on any old sidewalk to the particular path that we are on. The path, you might find, eventually guides you back into *actio* but with a renewed, more liberated heart. We can barely bear bearing the Good News!

Naomi Burton Stone, a friend of Thomas Merton's who became a friend of mine later in her life while we did retreats together, once gave a gift to me. Since I traveled a great deal and found myself walking down several different paths around the country, she sent me a little traveling companion: a teddy bear. It bore on its tag this simple message in her beautiful, clear handwriting, "The Gospel is true! We are all bear-ers of the Good News!" I can see her smile as I held the bear in her home in Maine.

One of the books Naomi told me a great deal about was Merton's *A Vow of Conversation*, which Merton asked Naomi to prepare for publication before he went on his journey to Asia where he sadly passed away. The book was a collection of journal entries and was a significant challenge for others. It was obvious that Merton was becoming comfortable expressing what was uncomfortable in his life, that which was, in fact, dissonant. Sometimes we might show more of ourselves than our friends would prefer. You might even sense their discomfort with your honesty. This was indeed the reaction of some trustees.

But in this story we also sense the spherical pattern of Lectio. I wonder if early composers of sacred scripture were ever nervous about what they passed onto us. I wonder if they ever feared their words would diminish our notion of the author, when, in fact, what it actually does is bring us into deeper communion with the very humanity of the author. In Lectio there is this movement of not only trusting your own experience with the Word but also trusting the experience of someone else. It is truly vernacular. Merton's work reflects an always honest movement, as he trusted Love's compass and stood before the Son.

When we are taken in by the Word, when we digest it and it manifests itself through us, we will take the Scriptures wherever we go. This journey, this *metanoia*—this moment of conversion where we let the light pierce through our mental and emotional patterns that do not serve us well—is an incredible, liberating encounter with Christ. But this only happens when we pause on the path and leave our hearts open to the word that has come to us, to the movement of Christ, "the Way." Then we will "rise and come into the field."

CHORDS AND SONGS, THREADS AND FABRICS

Chords—the beautiful arrangements of notes—form music that forms *us* as we listen. But we seem to live in a *discordant* time. We, with all our recent inventiveness, are facing the divisiveness and destructiveness of racism, of culture, and of the "false self" (as Merton called it). The order and ascendancy of chords sometimes seem broken, falling into dissonance, in this age of anxiety and disunity.

Art alerts us and calls us back "home" to a rich and solid dominant chord to which we might choose to return. As with Lectio, there is a great benefit in the ability to read notes and read words. But quite marvelously, each are "preformed" for us to "read" along as we listen.

Chords, at their best, arise in a creative space, as if for the first time. This coming together or weaving of notes, voices, instruments, environment, and, indeed, the silent anticipation of all who have gathered, causes a song to be born. This is the communal heart of church life that we "hear" in Lectio. It is (if we dare say it in a world where it seems we've been losing democracies), a particularly democratic practice. It is an inclusion of all voices present as the Word is heard.

St. John Henry Newman, a brilliant churchman and theologian, offered a sense that heart-to-heart conversation is really the core, or communal heart, of church life. His motto was *cor ad cor loquitur,* which means "heart speaks to heart." This is a tender spiritual image from a gentle man who shared his sharp mind with the Roman church. This "heart speaks to heart" notion is modeled for us in the Trinity: in the heart of Jesus Christ modeled for us in his ministry, the heart of the Father poured out in his Son, and the Spirit's manifestation in the hearts of people and pages of Scripture. All of this comes to us in Lectio Divina, and Trinity livens us together. *Sola voce* means that many voices are coming together in one voice, as we hear in Gregorian chant. This is the rising harmony (or even, at times, cacophony) in Lectio.

Newman and others offer a sense of ongoing revelation regarding the development of our core understandings of faith. This is close to the developmental theology we find early in the church teachings of St. Irenaeus. As churches institutionalized, we became somewhat fearful of "new expressions." But many of the original "developments" arose out of the initial *experiences* of the apostles, which now benefit all of us. Lectio is a continuation of this tradition, rooted in *experiencing* the Word. With Irenaeus's approach, if we were off the mark, it would also be a sign that we had fallen out of harmony with the faithful—we would have become discordant. The chords of our own music would be abrasive or in conflict with that which is in harmony by way of faith.

We see in early Christian theology, especially in Irenaeus, an expectation of beauty, a hope, a type of optimism for the growth and unfolding of the human person and all creation. This also then will be expressed in our human relationships and offer a positive perspective on our longing for—and moving ever more closely with and toward—our God. Religions of fear and threat do no good. When one is grace-filled, buoyed up by the delight and joy of love, growth is encouraged and understood as process.

In early theology, we see how relating is core to genuine spirituality. Out of these relationships we have the capacity to care for one another and reach out in service to our God and others. These early teachers celebrate a feminine insight. Relationships not only matter, but they are primary matter that life grows up and out of. Relationship-centered spirituality holds and welcomes other movements, like "Black lives matter," which remind us of our connectivity and the need to heal where relationships are discordant, destructive, and diseased. Like all holy words, "Black lives matter" hold within them all of us. We are moved to hold and reverence one another. The singularity and beauty of being a person of color is an invitation to all of us to understand our own signification, however manifest. As St. Irenaeus would let us know, all are "always blessed in Christ."

Might we pause and smile here? Yahweh is the first and final witness to this Song of Songs. We are loved and fully known. We love the fullness of the One who is always present—the note from which all music and theology cascades out into the world for those of us who have ears to hear and eyes to see.

The same language used to describe music is also used in weaving and fabrics. Like the compilation of chords into songs that change us, cords, fibers, filaments, threads, and yarn are sometimes shaped into ropes that can save lives. They become picnic tablecloths, grand tablecloths, and diapers. Chords and cords tie things together and draw things in. A chord holds a number of notes together. Cords provide a garment for me to wear in the winter. Chords and cords collect so much, but eventually it all harmonizes. Some of us begin to make jazz, not only with sound, but also with color and the very fabric of being human. Maybe you, too, love the movements, especially in music when extended sounds of dissonance seem discordant but then a whole harmony emerges and comes to a sweet resolve. It had been waiting for its moment to weave something to its completion— to the fullness of beauty.

You and I are already involved in the active learning, in coming to know, which is part of listening to the chords. As we listen, we awaken largesse—hopeful generosity—the reality that there is a superabundance for us and we didn't have to go collect it. It is given, presented to us, brought to us by the living God. Maybe this is why we hear in the story of the birth of Christ the choir of angels singing. This cannot be contained in prose only by itself.

Franciscan Lectio is a practice that is a multidimensional musical presentation. Its notes are often quiet, simple, and humble, but they can evolve into beautiful crescendos. We can feel them, even if we do not hear them. They all lend life to us. In our sacred reading at Mass, the ending of a passage is signified by the phrase "The Word of the Lord," like the period on an important sentence. The reader then might close the book, bow, and walk back to a ministerial chair or pew. In this empty space, we are invited to hear the Word again. What is the movement we sense within the hearts of the congregation? Within the art on the walls? Within the temple of our souls? What song is rising in our midst? What blanket is being woven?

The Word of the Lord, woven from the fabric of ourselves, strung by humility and humanity: these are the cords and ties that bring our hearts together and gather us in a circle. We sit at the feet of the Master. The very texture of our lives—the felt landscape, seascape, soul-scape—are woven of stories. Life, as is Lectio, is a story of stories—of "being here." It's a way of seeing the world as we begin to read the world. Yes, Adams and Eves, you and I, we are stories— stories of creation. Someone from history recalls us, and we are somehow alive where they are. The candle that burns before us is our story, as well as Christ's story, which is the heart of the cosmos.

INTER SIMPLICITY

The Lectio that was integrated into the Liturgy of the Hours in monastic communities was a cosmic care for creation and one another. Intimacy in Christ took them deeper into the vastness of the world they were called into. All of this, and the growth of their communal living, while on the road or semi-settled somewhere, was fueled by the Word of God—and interestingly, not normally by keepers of the institution! The Word kept them. They kept the Word. The hearing and reading of the Word, in its various forms, unified their community.

Francis's rule word for all of this is *inter*, which, in early Latin, means "be with," "be among," or "go among." Michael Blastic, OFM, a Franciscan scholar, opens up the meaning of this small word and its impact on the world as a guiding principle for Franciscans—a way of being, acting, and "going among." Francis encountered a living God beyond the rigidness of religion and political power structures—a God who invited him to a practice of prayer that would have him become one with the Word himself. The cross in San Damiano that, in many ways, guided him to the leper—to trees and to caves—led Francis to keep meeting the Cosmic Christ in the most intimate of ways, both through presence and people. So deep was Francis's experience with the Cosmic Christ that before he died he would receive the stigmata at La Verna. In Francis's own body, he received the most intimate sign of God's love for us. The San Damiano Cross that had sent him on his journey was now shining through him. As Bonaventure says of Francis, "When he (Francis) was speaking or proclaiming the Word, he became like a tongue proclaiming God's word." The core of his peacemaking was *inter*-focused—he went *among*, *with* and *in* the company of others, and peace rose out of his relational ministry, even at a divided time.

It takes a certain kind of presence to be *inter*-driven. It is difficult to truly be *among*, *with*, and *in* the company of others when the eyes of our hearts are elsewhere. Consider this intentional engagement with your own heart and mind as you choose to enter any setting. Are you open to people bringing more depth and beauty into your relationships? Much of our world, on the contrary, has taught us to enter, fully conscious of our status, role, opinions, and overall perception.

With an *inter* stance, we begin to be liberated from the captivity of our own egos. We no longer have to be right or make our opinion known. You might remember the story of St. Francis crossing over "enemy lines" during the Crusades to meet with the Sultan, al-Malik al-Kamil. He went there to preach the gospel and likely become a martyr. Francis was eventually ushered into the company of the Sultan, and the rapport that developed between the two was quite striking. It is said that their dialogue, or, as we would say here, *conversatio*, went on for days. The mutuality of the engagement of two men from different traditions (which were at war with one another, by the way) is given to us as an incarnation of *inter*, reflecting to us the dynamism of the Word. It was a non-dualistic movement (by both of them) in an age even more plagued by dualistic thinking than our own. To truly be *with* and *in* is to enter into a situation with peace, goodwill, and respect. Where in your life are you being invited to adopt an *inter* stance?

Francis's fundamental example of a way to be actively present to another—not at all passive—is significant in the Christian tradition. To trust the Word's power is really what we are about in this book. In both Francis and in his Lord and Savior, we witness incredibly simple, poor, and humble deliverers of God's Word. We read in Matthew's Gospel that the very Son of God turns first to prayer before he goes to his friends. Lectio is a wonderful complex (or complement) of different prayer styles that keep us in an ongoing engagement with this mysterious God in a world that is, at times, seemingly more mysterious. But this is the "God of heaven and earth" who chose to *inter*—to come among us. We have the opportunity to stand beside our fellow brothers and sisters (even if they are very different from us) in the garden once again.

PARADISO

When Francis was dying, he lay in a small garden near San Damiano called "Clare's Garden." We're told this is where he wrote Canticle of the Creatures, though he was weary, almost blind, near death, and had rodents climbing over him. It may have been a decrepit time in his life, but something rose up in his inner garden that waters the ground of our own gardens today. The San Damiano Cross—this cosmic piece to reconcile politics—was still spinning, even at a time when, as you might remember, the bishop of Assisi and the *podestà*, the mayor of Assisi, were in conflict. His cosmic canticle closes in a call for forgiveness and reconciliation, written at the request of his brothers who went and sang it in the square before the bishop's house.

Where is paradise? What is paradise? Where have holy women and men founded paradise? And are we finding it? Are we walking in paradise now?

Franciscans read the *activities* of Francis and Clare's lives and understand why both of them left us few words. There is more to read in both of their lives than an extended theological text could offer us. Their theology comes in stories. Where else do we find God? And where else might we find paradise?

Lectio is a doorway to, and a window on, a garden, a paradise. Lectio leads us into *paradiso,* an ancient image of a Persian garden that was a private space of solitude or intimate gathering, not so much a place of public proclamation or display. These gardens in Persia opened and evolved as a place beside royal dwellings. They were there for rest and relaxation, for conversation and engagement, for solitude and also heartfelt socializing. They were probably well-protected places with a substantial walls or dense hedges, likely also places for romance in their time—in the shadows of the trees, in the corners of speckled light. Cultivated plants were intentionally placed, and often arranged to reflect mythology. As we adopt an *inter* posture, how are we creating places of *paradiso* for others?

A gated garden often has internal gates and passages, labyrinths in which we would meander through and find our way, almost losing our way, and then finding our way again. Prayer would manifest in this organic setting, this garden, this paradise. There are similarities here to the Celtic sense of "thin spaces"—springs, groves, shorelines, or other spaces where one viscerally feels the convergence of heaven and earth. We begin to see (in other words, we begin to "read" or actively "do" Lectio) when we open up to the possibility of seeing Christ in the poor and the marginalized, even as they are put off by others. As it has been said in an old hymn, "God is all his creatures' home." This is the deep sense of abiding in a garden paradise.

The garden is the place of the beginning and the end. Francis's Canticle of the Creatures, which is one of the most cosmic of poems, helps us moderns know that when we are in love, nothing, no one, is an object but always in some way is a sister or a brother. It always takes a walk in the garden to come to know this. As Irenaeus wrote, "For just as God spoke then to Adam [in the garden] in the evening, as He searched for Him, so in the last days, with the same voice, He has visited the race of Adam, searching for it." This *paradiso* celebrates the primal beauty of our erotic self—the energy that draws us to walking and wandering deeper into our oneness. It is first and foremost and always a place for love. People might question whether or not we were ever really kicked out of the garden. But if that did happen, it may have been because we lapsed in our loving and missed understanding the core of ourselves. *As it was in the beginning, is now, and ever shall be, world without end, Amen.*

Through history people have always sought the oasis as a respite from their travels—a place lush with light and shade and fresh water. People of means and nobility have planted gardens, some beside grand houses and gathering places. This archetypical "garden activity" always seems to be the rediscovery of life's own activities and love itself. If it is love, it is always creative. *Eros* is active here—the creative energy of love that brings us into union. So as in the garden, so as also in this book, intimacy moves and grows.

The opportunity for intimacy is more than an idea. It is in and around us, especially in the gardens of our lives. That might be the corner of a porch or a chair in your living room but it depends on how we approach the place, the moment, and the people there.

Again and again, we need places to walk and wonder. It could be along a river gorge. It could be in a field, making camps with a friend. It could be in a dorm room with a Bible. It could be hiking through the woods during a time of grief. It could be before a mosaic or a crucifix.

Whatever those moments are, wherever those places are, they will take us deeper if we allow our heart and soul to travel with them. The garden that is actually the cosmos, under the tent, with its own pole that is Christ, is always a place of love. It has a compass.

THE MOVEMENT

"He is the image of the invisible God, the firstborn of all creation; for in him all things in heaven and on earth were created, things visible and invisible, whether thrones or dominions or rulers or powers—all things have been created through him and for him. He himself is before all things, and in him all things hold together. He is the head of the body, the church; he is the beginning, the firstborn from the dead, so that he might come to have first place in everything. For in him all

the fullness of God was pleased to dwell, and through him God

was pleased to reconcile to himself all things, whether on earth

or in heaven, by making peace through the blood of his cross."
— COLOSSIANS 1:15-20

When the barn where we found the wagon wheel was taken down to build our House of Peace—a beautiful building for prayer, meals, and visitors to stay, as well as for friars to live—we saved the wheel. I worked with the architect of the House of Peace to design a place over the fireplace in the common area where this wheel would hang. As I worked on the wheel, shaping and cleaning it for painting, it was as if I was being called to the privilege of enjoying what it already was—to not overdo anything artistically because the wheel had already been made by someone else and had done its job for years. It was, after all, the "old wheel from the barn." It was still rough and ragged in many ways, not unlike our own lives.

Rick and Tom, who finished the interior of our house, sandblasted the wheel before I began to paint it. Still with its own *patina*, apparent with this wheel was its handcraftedness. Beautiful as it was, it was made to carry a farm wagon (here at the end of the book, you might sense a contrast between what we think of as beautiful and what we think of as functional). Though one might look at the wheel from afar and see each spoke as similar and evenly spaced, up close the spokes had their own individuality. When I was oiling and painting the spokes, I knew where I was on the wheel by their differences. I knew where I was by the felt sense of what was there. Each spoke reflected the *haecceitas*—the beautiful uniqueness—of every individual creature.

What I realized as I painted was that the wheel was naturally evolving into a mandala. It was becoming a cosmic symbol, a convergence of the horizontal and vertical, the coming together of a cross in the One who is at the center of everything. As I took time painting each spoke, then moved on to the wheel itself and then, with help of others, added crossbeams, I knew I was connecting also with our sisters and brothers from south of the Equator who celebrate the Southern Cross, and others around the world who have mandalas and wheels that have great significance for them.

I used colors to express or relate to all of creation: blues, greens, browns, reds, and yellows. There was a feeling that fire was moving outward. The central image reflected the symbols of the Hopi people, the Western cross, the reflection cross, and the wheel of life in Hinduism and Buddhism. This *axis mundi*, an ancient name for Christ, the axle of the earth, is a reflection of Bonaventure's notion that Christ is the furnace of Jerusalem.

As I painted the wheel, I was reminded that I was being pointed toward the axle that is everywhere—*in* and *through* all that is. The wagon wheel is a monstrance. The San Damiano Cross is a monstrance. As my first Bible did in Devereux Hall on the campus of St. Bonaventure University, the wheel *revealed* something of God's mystery to me. It *demonstrated* a certain holding of the sacred; to be able to *gaze, consider, contemplate,* and *imitate* as we have named them in what we call the "Quadrants of St. Clare." We are all monstrances. We bear Christ. We receive and carry his life into the world. We don't just carry the ideas of Christ into the world; the gift we bear is Christ's life and love for the world. As this book comes to a close, may these words from St. Clare be a benediction for you wherever you might be on your journey:

What you hold, may you always hold.
What you do, may you do and never abandon.
But with swift pace, light step,
  unswerving feet,
  so that even your steps stir no dust,
go forward
  securely, joyfully, and swiftly,
on the path of prudent happiness,
  believing nothing
  agreeing with nothing
  which would dissuade you from this resolution
  or which would place a stumbling block for you on the way,
so that you may offer your vows to the Most High
in the pursuit of that perfection
to which the Spirit of the Lord has called you.

Lectio Divina opens us well beyond what we see. To learn to read the world—its wheels and wagons, its passages and places that seem hidden—is the activity of a practitioner of divine reading. You and I are invited to become students of a new way of being in the world, but, as has been said well before us, "there is no way to peace, peace *is* the way." I find more and more that seeing is the way to learning how to see even more.

Not long after my father died, I had a dream that still brightens my heart today. I was walking on the avenue that goes from our neighborhood to Lake Ontario, on my way to grammar school, passing by Lake Theater. My dad emerged with his arms up in the air, with the joy of someone who owned the whole world and wanted to give it away.

He cried out to me, "We are all going home together."

There seemed to be a moment's pause, and then, as he stepped closer, he said, with deepening joy and conviction, "Bill, we are all going home together."

And, as if the smile and voice wasn't loud enough the first time or the second, he said again, with a joyful shout that only my dad could, "Bill, we are all going home together!"

There was something about the words "home" and "together" that stayed with me as I woke that morning and has remained with me today. I accepted it as a calling I inherited from my father. I pass it onto you as we complete this book of reflections. Lectio invites us to join our homes and neighborhoods together and talk on our streets with one another. Might we again return to the mystery of our incarnational God who is still breathing life into the world through the Word?

This Christ, who seems asleep in the world, is awake. He wakes us up, too, so that we are ready to go again. Maybe your parents called out to you as mine did, "Rise and shine!" This simple phrase is an invitation to experience the beauty of the day. Lectio reclaims this enthusiasm. We rise to read all that comes before us. We become enamored again with beauty.

Our wagon wheel, in a sense, as it hangs in our common area over our fireplace, has been returned to its original beauty. From its first making, it was to carry life and what life needed. This practical object of farm, family, freedom, and now faith calls out to us for the same "return"—the journey that is ours with everyone and everything in the Alpha and the Omega.

Under this wheel—our mandala and monstrance for years now—we have shared sacred Scripture and practiced Lectio. We have enjoyed wine and beer. We have shared snacks before suppers prepared by those who have joined us. We've prayed, laughed, and cried. St. Irenaeus lets us know that we are each "handmade" and also connected to the center—the Christ who went on before us to Galilee. We are formed by our Creator's hands and shaped for a wonderful purpose, which is to "fit" beside others—to stand together and form and shape this whole wheel of a world so that it might do what wheels want to do: "move on down the road!"

So much can seem to impede our journey, to block or broadside our way, and yet, we are on our way. Christ is our way. The lives we live truly are pilgrimages. Sometimes we are strangers in a strange land. Sometimes we feel we are beside strangers, which is a new and important experience. We are moved to keep walking and perhaps sometimes to take a new path. When our lives feel rough and ragged, life is still going on if we have eyes to see, if we are doing Lectio with all of life and all the world from our inner place of blessed creativity. Out from the center—the core, the axle of the world, the One given by God who is the ordering of all things, the One who would carry the wagon and its load—we are called forth. Why? So that each of us, all of us, with our mixed and wonderfully gifted personalities— spokes out from the axle—all carry the wagon, helping to move the world, as we, in the Word, move with one another.

THE GLORY OF GOD IS A HUMAN PERSON FULLY ALIVE. ST. IRENAEUS

Each of us is a spoke.   Together we are the wheel.

ACKNOWLEDGMENTS

few years ago, Murray Bodo, OFM, invited me to "write your own *Itinerarium Mentis in Deum*." Bruno Barnhart, OSB Cam, of New Camaldoli Hermitage in Big Sur, California, urged me to do something similar. "Write a book from within the Franciscan wisdom tradition," he told me. I am grateful to these men and other Franciscan women and men for how their rich spiritual practices have informed me.

I am blessed to have lived in a community of friars and sisters at Mt. Irenaeus for nearly forty years, including Joseph Kotula, OFM, Louis McCormick, OFM, and Kevin Kriso, OFM, as well as Michael Fenn. Other women and men in ministry and leadership with us have been mentors to me as well. Our dear brother, Daniel Hurley, OFM, gave me my deepest and most enjoyable lifelong model of being Franciscan. As he once said, "I love my God, and my God loves me." Friars at St. Bonaventure University—notably Gervase White, Evan Banks, Roy Gasnick, Felton Robinson, and David Wallace— showed me the riches of the Franciscan Way.

Stephen and I give special thanks to Michelle Marcellin who has been essential to this book; generous with her time and skills, she has supported us through transcription after transcription and editing. Ann McCarthy offered an honest and helpful review and an edit of this early work, as she always has with my writing. Tony Bannon prodded me with his insights. Bob Cancalosi, Joel Serra, and Greg Licamele were inspiring to me as they participated in this and other media ventures. I am especially grateful to Paul Kugler for our long relationship, counsel, and mentoring (as well as his insights) when I read to him early sections of the manuscript.

Marcia Marcus Kelly (and her husband, Jack) brought me into friendship with her uncle, Robert Lax, whose blessing and work remains in me. Naomi Burton Stone became a dear friend with whom I shared many conversations, some of which were about her own work with her friend Thomas Merton; through this, she became a great encourager of our life at Mt. Irenaeus.

Following a presentation at a Merton conference a few years ago, Stephen Copeland and I fell into another's company, engaging in a sidewalk "conversatio." Our minds were still on fire from what we heard, as Stephen said to me, "Father Dan, you need to write a book, and I will work on it with you!" Thus began an exceptionally blessed collaboration and graced encounter with Stephen, a gifted writer, a very skilled composer, and an assembler of these texts. Both of us—men of many words—learned a great deal together in trying to express that which is beyond words.

My life has been blessed by Stephen and so many other sisters and brothers in the Franciscan family and those who I have met along the way. Ultimately this book is about being open to one's journey, to listen to the Word. May you listen deeply, and may your journey be blessed.

"RECIPES" FOR LECTIO

Having taken time with this book, and reflecting on your life, you know now that Lectio is a full meal. It is far more than only hors d'oeuvres or dessert, yet it will often include an attractive "side salad." We might say Lectio is a table set for us, as the Psalmist invites us to "taste and see the goodness of the Lord." As is carved in the wood beams over our supper table in our Holy Peace home at the Mountain, "They recognized him in the breaking of bread."[77] So, the metaphor of recipes—and the process of baking and cooking—might be helpful in a world that is truly hungry. This is why we share the Word and the bread of life with each other. This is also why we seek the ingredients for Lectio in our daily lives. This prepares us to go cook and enjoy the table of fellowship. Either in solitude or with others who gather, God joins us at the table, as we prepare ourselves to enter the world in a new way.

Lectio of the Desert: We owe this banquet of Lectio to our Desert Fathers and Mothers, who left the "table" of their own culture and their ways of life to find meaning in the desert. They, as we, desired to change their eating habits and looked for healthier ones. Now, thanks to monastic life, we still have the basic ingredients, fresh from faith's oven of traditional Lectio. These practices fed hungry people in the desert long ago: *Oratio* (for prayer to open), *Lectio* (to read), *Meditatio* (to meditate), *Contemplatio* (to welcome contemplation as it arises), and *Actio* (the impact and import of the Word itself which calls us to action). To look toward a more natural diet might also suggest some of what we are doing when we talk about recipes for Lectio.

Lectio of St. Clare: You may have your own place of entering our early conversation with Francis and Clare. St. Clare's practice before the San Damiano Cross can influence our own Lectio practices, as we *Gaze, Consider, Contemplate,* and *Imitate.* See the "Quadrants of St. Clare" section toward the beginning of Part I, as well as the introductions for each quadrant in this book.

Lectio on the Road: For over thirty years, I've been privileged to travel around our country with Joe Flanagan, the director of Alumni Services for St. Bonaventure University. Often we are joined by Br. Joe Kotula, OFM, and a team of two to four young women and men—undergraduates of our university. This is our "On the Road" ministry, where we come together as both pilgrims and strangers. As St. Peter tells us, pilgrims and strangers know more when we sit down at a common table, then take that nourishment into our daily lives and begin together to face the needs of our world that is hungry for justice, love, and peace. See the section "Communal Lectio" toward the end of Part I and consider how you might take these recipes on the road of your own life.

We certainly don't want to take the fun away from you of shaping and experimenting with your own recipes for Lectio Divina. Lectio is not random but is rich in spontaneity and depth as the spirit of God surprises us so that we also surprise one another when we "cook Lectio." If you need some more ideas, consider practicing Lectio as you walk (see the section "Sidewalk Lectio" toward the end of Part IV); Lectio as stance (see the "Sentinels" section at the end of Part III); Lectio of the Jesuits (Observe, Judge, Act); Lectio of the Mountain (Remember, Reflect, Respond); the Four S's of Lectio (Solitude, Silence, Simplicity, Service); or the Four W's of Lectio (Watch, Wonder, Wait, Work). All you need are ingredients. What you cook is up to you.

At Mt. Irenaeus, in the back hills of Allegheny County, we've learned a lot about this courage to create—to find new ways with each other. I remember with great affection when the house was full of students and, in particular, a couple of our men's overnights when we came upon a recipe for "mountain potatoes." Many of the young men had never cooked before. Yet, with a large basin in front of us, some chopped potatoes, carrots, and onions while others reached into the refrigerator for sauces. Stirring this together, enjoying the freedom of discovery, we found the willingness we had among us to work together. This blossomed again later in the evening when we took a walk in the woods and entered our chapel in silence to now open God's Word in each other's company and enter once again as earlier in a form of "communal Lectio."

St. Clare baked and broke bread with her sisters and with others in the small town of Assisi. She baked food for the poor and the rich at the same time, knowing that they were all hungry. You already know what you long for. Each of us is hungry. The ancients have offered us a recipe. Together now but also in solitude, let us believe that we are called to bake the bread and cook the meal with one another, and let us especially remember that Francis and Clare and our world today ask us to always be willing to welcome others to our "table of plenty."

OTHER RECOMMENDED RESOURCES

1. Barnhart, Bruno. *Second Simplicity: The Inner Shape of Christianity* (Mahwah, NJ: Paulist Press, 1999).

2. Barnhart, Bruno. *The Future of Wisdom: Toward a Rebirth of Sapiential Christianity* (Rhinebeck, NY: Monkfish, Second edition, 2018).

3. Barrows, Anita. *Rilke's Book of Hours: Love Poems to God* (New York: Riverhead Books, 1996).

4. Berry, Thomas. *The Sacred Universe: Earth, Spirituality, and Religion in the Twenty-First Century* (New York: Columbia University Press, 2009.

5. Bodo, Murray. *Clare: A Light in the Garden* (Cincinnati, OH: Franciscan Media, 1979).

6. Bodo, Murray. *The Way of St. Francis* (New York: Doubleday; 1st edition, 1984).

7. Burton-Christie, Douglas. *The Word in the Desert: Scripture and the Quest for Holiness in Early Christian Monasticism* (Oxford, UK: Oxford University Press USA, 1993).

8. Cannato, Judy. *Radical Amazement: Contemplative Lessons from Black Holes, Supernovas, and Other Wonders of the Universe* (Notre Dame, IN: Ave Maria Press, 2006).

9. Cannato, Judy. *Field of Compassion: How the New Cosmology Is Transforming Spiritual Life* (Notre Dame, IN: Sorin Books, 2010).

10. Carney, Margaret. *Light of Assisi: The Story of Saint Clare* (Cincinnati, OH: Franciscan Media, 2021)

11. Casey, Michael. *Sacred Reading: The Ancient Art of Lectio Divina* (Chicago: Triumph Books, 1996).

12. Cunningham, Lawrence. *Francis of Assisi: Performing the Gospel of Life.* (Dulles, VA: Eerdmans, 2004).

13. Cunningham, Lawrence. *Thomas Merton: Spiritual Master, The Essential Writings* (Mahwah, NJ: Paulist Press, 1992).

14. Daloz Parks, Sharon. *Big Questions, Worthy Dreams: Mentoring Emerging Adults in Their Search for Meaning, Purpose, and Faith* (Minneapolis: Fortress Press, 2019).

15. Delio, Ilia. *The Humility of God: A Franciscan Perspective* (Cincinnati, OH: St. Anthony Messenger Press, 2006).

16. Delio, Ilia. *The Unbearable Wholeness of Being* (Ossining, NY: Orbis, 2013).

17. Edwards, Denis. *Jesus and the Cosmos* (Mahwah, NJ: Paulist Press, 2004).

18. Freeman, Laurence. *Jesus the Teacher Within* (Norwich, UK: Hymns Ancient & Modern, 2010).

19. Frugoni, Chiara. *Francis of Assisi: A Life* (New York: Continuum, 1998).

20. Haule, John. *The Ecstasies of St. Francis: The Way of Lady Poverty.* (Lindisfarne, UK, Lindisfarne Books, 2001).

21. Hausherr, Irénée. *The Name of Jesus* (Collegeville, MN: Cistercian Publications, 1978).

22. Hayes, Zachary. *The Hidden Center* (St. Bonaventure, NY: Franciscan Institute, 1992).

23. Hillman, James. *The Thought of the Heart and the Soul of the World* (Washington, DC: Spring Publications, 1992).

24. Iriarte de Aspurz, Lázaro. *The Franciscan Calling*, trans. Sister Carole Marie Kelly, OSF (Quincy, IL: Franciscan Herald Press, 1974).

25. Kilcourse, George. *Ace of Freedoms: Thomas Merton's Christ* (Notre Dame, IN: University of Notre Dame Press, 1993).

26. Lane, Beldon C. *The Solace of Fierce Landscapes: Exploring Desert and Mountain Spirituality* (Oxford, UK: Oxford University Press, Eighth edition, 2007).

27. Lax, Robert. *Love Had a Compass: Journals and Poetry* (New York: Grove Press, Reprint edition, 2019).

28. Macy, Joanna; Young, Molly. *Coming Back to Life: Practices to Reconnect Our Lives, Our World* (Gabriola Island, BC: New Society Publishers, 1998).

29. McGinn, Bernard. *The Flowering of Mysticism: Men and Women in the New Mysticism (1200-1350)* (New York: Herder & Herder, Second edition, 1998).

30. Merton, Thomas. *Contemplation in a World of Action* (New York: The Catholic Book Club, 1986).

31. Merton, Thomas. *No Man Is an Island* (Boston, MA: Mariner Books, 2002).

32. Merton, Thomas. *The Collected Poems of Thomas Merton* (New York: New Directions, 1980.

33. Merton, Thomas. *The Inner Experience: Notes on Contemplation* (New York: Harper, 2004).

34. Mueller, Joan. *Clare of Assisi: The Letters to Agnes* (Collegeville, MN: Liturgical Press, 2003)

35. Murphy, Roland E. *The Tree of Life: An Exploration of Biblical Wisdom Literature* (Grand Rapids, MI: Eerdmans, Third edition, 2002).

36. Nhat Hahn, Thich. *The Heart of Understanding: Commentaries on the Prajnaparamita Heart Sutra* (Berkeley, CA: Parallax Press, 1988).

37. O'Donohue, John. *Beauty: The Invisible Embrace* (New York: Harper Perennial, 2005).

38. Parks, Sharon. *The Critical Years: The Young Adult Search for a Faith to Live By* (New York: Harper & Row; 1st edition, 1986).

39. Plotkin, Bill. *Nature and the Human Soul: Cultivating Wholeness and Community in a Fragmented World* (Novato, CA: New World Library, Illustrated edition, 2007).

40. Rilke, Rainer Maria. *Rilke's Book of Hours: Love Poems to God*, trans. Anita Barrows and Joanna Macy (New York: Riverhead Books, 1996).

41. Rohr, Richard. *Eager to Love: The Alternative Way of Francis of Assisi* (Cincinnati, OH: Franciscan Media, 2016).

42. Rohr, Richard. *Falling Upward: A Spirituality for the Two Halves of Life* (Hoboken, NJ: Jossey-Bass, 2012).

43. Rohr, Richard. *Immortal Diamond: The Search for Our True Self* (Hoboken, NJ: Jossey-Bass, 2013).

44. Schillebeeckx, Edward. *The Church with a Human Face: A New and Expanded Theology of Ministry* (New York: Crossroad, 1985).

45. Shannon, William H. *Thomas Merton's Paradise Journey: Writings on Contemplation* (New York: Continuum, 2000).

46. Steenberg, M. C. *Of God and Man: Theology as Anthropology from Irenaeus to Athanasius* (Edinburgh, UK: T&T Clark, 2009).

47. Sweeney, Jon. *Francis and Clare: A True Story* (Brewster, MA: Paraclete Press, Illustrated edition, 2014).

48. Urs von Balthasar, Hans. *Scandal of the Incarnation: Irenaeus Against the Heresies* (San Francisco: Ignatius Press, Second Edition, 1990).

49. Vauchez, André. *Francis of Assisi: The Life and Afterlife of a*

Medieval Saint (New Haven, CT: Yale University Press; First Paperback Edition, 2013).

50. Von Matt, Leonard; Hauser, Water. *St Francis Of Assisi* (London, UK: Longmans, 1956).

51. Wilber, Ken. *A Brief History of Everything* (Boulder, CO: Shambhala, 2001).

52. Wilber, Ken. *Integral Spirituality: A Startling New Role for Religion in the Modern and Postmodern World* (Boulder, CO: Shambhala, Reprint edition, 2007).

53. Wilber, Ken. *The Marriage of Sense and Soul: Integrating Science and Religion* (New York: Harmony, 1999).

NOTES

1 The January 2022 article in *Common Wheel,* "'Lived from the Heart,'" features Kenneth Woodward's interview with Bernard McGinn, who makes the point that any theology today needs to be mystical: https://www.commonwealmagazine .org/lived-heart. We have often mistakenly limited mystical practice and mystical theology to the realm of the monastery. McGinn, as others here, makes the point that Franciscan theology is vernacular.

2 In *The Word in the Desert* by Douglas Burton-Christie (Oxford, UK: Oxford University Press, 1993) and *The Word* by Michael Casey (pp. 8, 9, 13, 38, 39, 71), both authors take us into the truth that the Word is an event. At the essential level of theologizing, as in the desert, spirituality does not become a subset to theology. Casey, as a Trappist might, opens us to mindfulness, which is being rediscovered in the West but was never lost in the desert wisdom.

3 Like many of us who have gone on the journey to find ourselves, both Murray Bodo and Richard Rohr open up for us in their biographies of Francis and Clare (see the "Other Recommended Resources" pages) a truly human—what we Franciscans would call "incarnational"—journey that gives us hope for our own. Every page in this book is somehow either touched or inspired by them.

4 From Robert Lax's "Circus of the Sun" in *Love Had a Compass* (New York: Grove Press, 1996).

5 Ewert Cousins, a scholar of St. Bonaventure's *The Soul's Journey into God,* addresses the importance of axial and pre-axial ages at the beginning of his book *Christ of the 21st Century* (New York: Continuum, 1994), integrating the work of authors like Jaspers. The task of our book is outlined in this sentence from Cousins: "The human race as a whole—all the diverse cultures and the religions—must face these problems squarely. In this Second Axial Period we must rediscover the dimensions of consciousness of the spirituality of the primal peoples of the pre-Axial Period."

6 In his book *A Brief History of Everything* (Boulder, CO: Shambhala, 2001), Ken Wilber takes us into a reconsideration of the way we configure learning meaning and its expression. Mandalas, wheels, spirals, and spinning objects are found in every ancient and developing spirituality. When I was first reading Wilber, I was

struck by his understanding of quadrants as a rich way of seeing things organized and in relationship with one another. The underlying theology that Wilber does not attempt to articulate is some of what we are working on here, and we invite you to continue your own work as you spin, dance, and circle.

7 See James Hillman's *The Thought of the Heart, and the Soul of the World* (Washington, DC: Spring Publications, 1998).

8 *The New Dictionary of Theology* (Downers Grove, IL: IVP Academic, 1988).

9 *The Dictionary of the Bible* (New York: Touchstone, reprint edition, 1995).

10 Robert Lax's 1959 "The Circus of the Sun" is a seminal poem that is central to what we are doing in this book and is quoted thoroughly throughout. The poem's title reflects Francis of Assisi's "Canticle of the Sun" and follows a day in a traveling circus, inviting readers into an intimate cosmology.

11 Colossians 3:11.

12 Writes T. S. Eliot in his poem "Little Gidding," *What we call the beginning is often the end / And to make an end is to make a beginning. / The end is where we start from.*

13 Hebrews 4:12: "Indeed, the word of God is living and effective, sharper than any two-edged sword, penetrating even between soul and spirit, joints and marrow, and able to discern reflections and thoughts of the heart."

14 John McKenzie's writings about *dabar,* which means "act" or "activity"—the Word as event—in his *Dictionary of the Bible* invite us to rediscover the pedagogy of the Hebrew people.

15 (Cincinnati, OH: Franciscan Media, 2012). Other recommended books by Murray Bodo: *Tales of St. Francis: Ancient Stories for Contemporary Living* (New York: Image, 1988) and *Clare: A Light in the Garden* (Cincinnati, OH: Franciscan Media, 1979).

16 From "Day of a Stranger" by Thomas Merton: "So perhaps I have an obligation to preserve the stillness, the silence, the poverty, the virginal point of pure nothingness which is at the center of all other loves. I attempt to cultivate this plant without comment in the middle of the night and water it with psalms and prophecies in silence. It becomes the most rare of all the trees in the garden, at once the primordial paradise tree, the axis mundi, the cosmic axle, and the Cross. . . . There is only one such tree. It cannot be multiplied. It is not interesting."

17 See Andre Vauchez's translation of *The Three Companions,* which was written by three of Francis's friars who recalled their time with him.

18 Acts 17:28: "For 'In him we live and move and have our being,' as even some of your own poets have said, 'For we too are his offspring.'"

19 Robert Lax's journals and poetry in *Love Had a Compass* (New York: Grove Press, 1996) show his evolution as a poet and feature some of his best work.

20 See Eric Osborn, *Irenaeus of Lyons* (Cambridge, UK: Cambridge University Press, 2005).

21 On sabbatical I came upon *Solace and Fierce Landscapes* (Oxford, UK: Oxford University Press, 2007) by Belden Lane, a Presbyterian theologian who taught at St. Louis University. I was immediately moved by his manner of doing theology, opening the reader to biographic moments and ancient spiritual journeys that were stirring also in him. He, like other authors noted here, lent their own liberation to me.

22 I suggest a dynamic reading of Clare's letters and our quadratic understanding of them, not unlike how we might experience Leonardo da Vinci's "Vitruvian Man," a figure of a man inscribed in a circle and square, understood to be an autobiographical image of da Vinci but also a "Renaissance Man" who is also "the Christ." The quadrants rise up off the page and invite us to experience the dynamic of his drawing.

23 In *Clare of Assisi: The Letters to Agnes* (Collegeville, MN: Liturgical Press, 2003), Joan Mueller, OFS, a Franciscan scholar, offers us a real-life picture of Clare and her communication with Agnes. Their communication was beautiful, profound, and personal, though they never met face to face. Mueller, in her way of lending us the clarity of Clare's pure and certain theology, helps us believe that transparency and intimacy can truly happen over a distance—that power and position and place do not reign over it.

24 May, whose work is so rich and relatable, continually invites us into the power of slowing in our everyday lives. Consider meditating upon this quote from *The Wisdom of Wilderness* (New York: HarperOne, 2007) and adopting this posture, or stance, in the scenes of your own life: "I relax again as I drive to the mountain . . . feeling an encircling warmth, more and more. I feel it like a caress, and I sense myself responding to it, wanting to be welcoming myself, wanting to gently enter gentleness, desiring to be as hospitable to the wilderness as it is to me. . . . A great relief for a psychiatrist, I have been beautifully, exquisitely mystified."

25 1 Peter 2:4–5: "Come to him, a living stone, rejected by human beings but chosen and precious in the sight of God, and, like living stones, let yourselves be built into a spiritual house to be a holy priesthood to offer spiritual sacrifices acceptable to God through Jesus Christ."

26 In his strikingly contemporary book *Francis of Assisi: A Model of Human Liberation* (Ossining, NY: Orbis Books, 25th Anniversary edition, 2006), Leonardo Boff (who was at one time a Franciscan and is still a Franciscan theologian) brings Francis and our Franciscan way into play with the oppressive systems of our world today.

27 Judy Cannato's *Radical Amazement* (Notre Dame, IN: Ave Maria Press, 2006) and *Field of Compassion* (Notre Dame, IN: Sorin Books, 2010) open up the cosmology of our Christian faith. Helping us to enter into a place with Christ, Cannato invites us—in her wonderful, accessible writing—to marvel over everything.

28 Ewert Cousins unfolds in his book *Christ of the 21st Century* a cosmology that engages theology as well as the social and psychological sciences. He speaks from the heart of Bonaventurian theology in this postmodern time when many of our institutions are either broken or under reconstruction. His work has influenced many of the authors quoted in this book, particularly Sr. Ilia Delio, OSF, an essential and outstanding voice for multiple theological questions today. He lifts up in profoundly hopeful ways our Christology and how it has an enriched our understanding of axial times.

29 Ephesians 1:17–19: [I pray] "that the God of our Lord Jesus Christ, the Father of glory, may give you a spirit of wisdom and revelation resulting in knowledge of him. May the eyes of [your] hearts be enlightened, that you may know what is the hope that belongs to his call, what are the riches of glory in his inheritance among the holy ones, and what is the surpassing greatness of his power for us who believe, in accord with the exercise of his great might."

30 Artist Meg Fish Saligman is creating a mural on the side of a campus building at Jamestown Community College in Olean, New York, the hometown of Robert Lax, based on his poem "Circus of the Sun." Philip Glass's 2021 opera, *Circus Days and Nights*, is also based on Lax's poem.

31 In *Nature and the Human Soul* (Novato, CA: New World Library, 2007), Bill Plotkin helps us, in his descriptiveness, to find and discover in our dreams and our own modeling some of what we don't find in the narrowing of our imaging and imagining. He hosts vision quests, where he helps stir people to see things as they are through fasting and encountering silence.

32 See *Aesthetic Theology in the Franciscan Tradition* by Xavier Seubert (London, UK: Routledge, 2019), *The Visible and the Invisible* by Maurice Merleau-Ponty (Evanston, IL: Northwestern University Press, 1968), and *Ideas: General*

Introduction to Pure Phenomenology by Edmund Husserl (Lanham, MD: Routledge, 2012).

33 2 Timothy 2:8–9: "Remember Jesus Christ, raised from the dead, a descendant of David: such is my gospel, for which I am suffering, even to the point of chains, like a criminal. But the word of God is not chained."

34 Consider these lines from Mary Oliver's "Morning in a New Land," which, echoing T. S. Eliot, help us to form our contemplative stance in Lectio, where we see through new eyes again and again: *"And under the trees, beyond time's brittle drift, / I stood like Adam in his lonely garden / On that first morning, shaken out of sleep, / Rubbing his eyes, listening, parting the leaves, / Like tissue on some vast, incredible gift."*

35 See *Conjectures of a Guilty Bystander* (New York: Image, 1968), 158.

36 1 Corinthians 3:16: "Do you not know that you are God's temple and that God's Spirit dwells in you?"

37 In his book on Franciscan Christology, *The Hidden Center* (St. Bonaventure, NY: Franciscan Institute, St. Bonaventure University, 1992), Zachary Hayes shows how Bonaventure's work is the seedbed of many other theologies; that the unitive nature in the "hidden center" is the *axis mundi*, the core.

38 In *Centering in Poetry, Pottery, and Person* (Middletown, CT: Wesleyan University Press, 1989) M. C. Richards, with wonderful humor and wisdom, helps us look at our own experiences of feeling "broken" or "poorly shaped," a familiar journey to each of us. This author had a profound effect on me as I began first looking at centering. She began her life in literature and completed graduate work in ceramics. She taught pottery, while at the same time she was able to pass on modalities and understandings of meditation and centering.

39 1 John 3:2: "Beloved, we are God's children now; what we will be has not yet been revealed. What we do know is this: when he is revealed, we will be like him, for we will see him as he is."

40 Colossians 1:15–17: "He is the image of the invisible God, the firstborn of all creation; for in him were created all things in heaven and on earth, the visible and invisible, whether thrones or dominions or principalities or powers—all things were created through him and for him. He is before all things, and in him all things hold together."

41 Maria Harris (*Teaching and Religious Imagination* [Harper San Francisco, 1991]) and her husband, Gabriel Moran (*The Act of Teaching: Reflections on a Basic*

Human Act [San Francisco: FolioAvenue Publishing Service, 2020]), as well as other authors like Bill Plotkin, Sharon Parks, and David Abrams, uncover ancient ways of coming to know and discover the relevance of these pedagogies today. St. Bonaventure, one of the great teachers in our Franciscan tradition, highlights his own conscious wrestling with coming to know in his prologue to *The Soul's Journey into God* (see "Lectio and the Senses" in Part II).

42 As Pierre Teilhard de Chardin, SJ, told Gabriele Maria Allegra, OFM, in *My Conversations with Teilhard de Chardin on the Primacy of Christ* (Chicago: Franciscan Herald Press, 1971), "Sacred scripture teaches us the most profound truths in the most simple words. . . . Further, it is idyl or cosmic drama. The world has meaning only in Christ. I have said 'idyl or cosmic drama' because one of the objections raised against my theory is that I deny the drama, the reality of human tragedy, and allow myself to be driven by a sort of naive optimism. But then, what about St. Francis and his canticle of the sun? Is he not an optimist? Does not the revealed doctrine of Christ as Alpha and Omega encourage all of us to be optimists?"

43 Pope Francis and popes before him have asked us to approach the world in this way by "reading the signs of the times." This is contemporary Catholic practice of contemplation and justice.

44 Michael Blastic, OFM, situates *conversatio* in the habit of Franciscans, which we call going "among" others. This is three-hundred-and-sixty-degree vulnerability of engagement to both assimilate life as it is and thus be able to proclaim the good news.

45 A cosmic sense of God shows up throughout Paul's writings, as referenced here in Ephesians 3:14–19: "For this reason I bow my knees before the Father, from whom every family in heaven and on earth takes its name. I pray that, according to the riches of his glory, he may grant that you may be strengthened in your inner being with power through his Spirit, and that Christ may dwell in your hearts through faith, as you are being rooted and grounded in love. I pray that you may have the power to comprehend, with all the saints, what is the breadth and length and height and depth, and to know the love of Christ that surpasses knowledge, so that you may be filled with all the fullness of God." This notion is also reflected in Philippians 2:5–11, Colossians 1:15–20, as well as Joanine literature, particularly 1 John 1 and John 1.

46 See Lawrence S. Cunningham's excellent compilation of Merton's writings in *Thomas Merton: Spiritual Master* (Mahwah, NJ: Paulist Press, 1992).

47 Ephesians 1:17–19 was a favorite passage of St. Bonaventure's.

48 See Thich Nhat Hanh's *The Heart of Understanding: Commentaries on the Prajnaparamita Heart Sutra* (Berkeley, CA: Parallax Press, revised edition, 2009).

49 Ilia Delio, OSF, whose wisdom permeates this book, invites us into the wonder of Franciscan cosmology in her books *The Unbearable Wholeness of Being* (Ossining, NY: Orbis, 2013), *Making All Things New* (Orbis, 2015), and *The Humility of God: A Franciscan Perspective* (Cincinnati, OH: St. Anthony Messenger Press, 2015). There is an important correspondence between Delio's writing and research and what I've been writing about in the arena of Lectio. As she writes in *Making All Things New*, "As the principle of attraction toward more being, love is the affinity of being with Being and a general principle of all cosmic life. Teilhard writes that 'love is the most universal, most tremendous, and the most mysterious of the cosmic forces.' The whole of reality from the lowest to the highest is covenanted, united in a bond of love." Delio continually reminds us in her work that "God and the world are in process together . . . the world continually participates in God and God in the world."

50 See Teilhard de Chardin's *The Phenomenon of Man* (New York: Harper Perennial, 1976, originally translated in 1959).

51 Jeremiah 14:9b.

52 See Zachary Hayes, *The Hidden Center: Spirituality and Speculative Christology in St. Bonaventure* (St. Bonaventure, NY: Franciscan Institute, 2000).

53 Lax introduced Merton to the hills and valleys, and today there is a clearing in the wooded hills on the other side of the Allegheny known as "Merton's Heart" (shown in the sketch on page 181) where he is said to have often spent time reflecting. Both Lax and Merton were going through significant transformations and openness to life and creation. Merton was especially drawn to Blake, whose works were the basis of his Master's Degree at Columbia.

54 This is a quote often attributed to (and somewhere found in the legends of) St. Francis, though scholars have been unable to identify the specific source.

55 See the "Sentinels" section in Part III.

56 In 1971, Leonard Bernstein, a great composer, conductor, pianist, and teacher of both classical and contemporary works, presented *MASS*, inspired by the Catholic Church's traditional Mass. Bernstein pivots from where the Mass stands.

57 Ephesians 2:19.

58 "Rain and the Rhinoceros" was first published in 1965 by *Holiday,* one of the most popular magazines in the United States between 1946 and 1977.

59 John 14:6.

60 Another mantra that arose during that time was "Throw everything into the fire of God's love."

61 David Abram, author of *Spell of the Sensuous* (New York: Vintage, 1997) and Robert Bellah, author of *Religion in Human Evolution* (Cambridge, MA: Belknap Press, 2011), both speak of how our ancient forbears listened to nature's sounds (especially to bird calls) for alerts—both for safety and for concern, for weather and for food. We, too, are writing a book about the human journey, a book about survival.

62 Isaiah 55:12.

63 I hope you're beginning to sense at this point that a major theme of this book, albeit subtle, is unlocking the sacred feminine within our world, the Word, and ourselves.

64 In *The Flowering of Mysticism* (Pearl River, NY: Herder & Herder, 1998), Bernard McGinn talks about Franciscan theology as a vernacular experience rather than a monastic tradition. With his perspective on Franciscan theology and its place in relationship to other theologies that have grown up over time, he notes that Franciscan theology is a vernacular theology and mystical by way of its place in the world.

65 Gerard Manley Hopkins, a great Jesuit poet, in a number of his poems picks up on the deep theological intuition of Scotus.

66 Colossians 1:15–20a: "He is the image of the invisible God, the firstborn of all creation. For in him were created all things in heaven and on earth, the visible and the invisible, whether thrones or dominions or principalities or powers; all things were created through him and for him. He is before all things, and in him all things hold together. He is the head of the body, the church. He is the beginning, the firstborn from the dead, that in all things he himself might be preeminent. For in him all the fullness was pleased to dwell, and through him to reconcile all things for him, making peace by the blood of his cross."

67 In *The Future of Wisdom: A Rebirth of Sapiential Christianity* (Rhinebeck, NY: Monkfish, 2018), Fr. Bruno Barnhart, a Camaldoli monk, has done us a great service in his primary writings around wisdom. Some years ago, he encouraged

me to write from the Franciscan disposition, which I've attempted to do in this book. He, too, reflects on four historical moments and four movements. Quadrant imagery and spiral imagery appear in his work and in that of others.

68 See *Conjectures of a Guilty Bystander* (New York: Image, 1968).

69 As Richard Rohr, OFM, makes clear in his book *The Naked Now* (New York: Crossroad, 2009), the human tendency is to slip into dualistic thinking and scapegoating. Lectio and contemplation guide us into non-dualism—an awareness of our interconnectedness with the world, which includes those who seem most different from us.

70 See Pulitzer Prize-winning Annie Dillard's *Holy the Firm* (New York: Harper Perennial, revised edition, 1998).

71 Romans 8:25: "But if we hope for what we do not see, we wait with endurance."

72 Matthew 10:8: "Cure the sick, raise the dead, cleanse lepers, cast out demons. Without cost you have received; without cost you are to give."

73 Matthew 11:29–30: "Take my yoke upon you and learn from me, for I am meek and humble of heart, and you will find rest for yourselves. For my yoke is easy, and my burden light."

74 1 John 3:2: "Beloved, we are God's children now; what we will be has not yet been revealed. We do know that when it is revealed, we shall be like him, for we shall see him as he is."

75 In *Soulcraft: Crossing into the Mysteries of Nature and Psyche* (Novato, CA: New World Library, 2003), Bill Plotkin offers us insights that are related to Ken Wilber's but more by modality as he plunges into a deep understanding of post-Jungian psychology. A rich writer with a simulating sense of spirituality, he saturates each page with what we might call integration.

76 See Henri Nouwen's *Spiritual Formation: Following the Movements of the Spirit* (New York: HarperOne, 2010).

77 Luke 24:33-35: "They got up and returned at once to Jerusalem. There they found the Eleven and those with them, assembled together and saying, 'It is true! The Lord has risen and has appeared to Simon.' Then the two told what had happened on the way, and how Jesus was recognized by them when he broke the bread."

Visit Mt. Irenaeus at
www.mountainonline.org

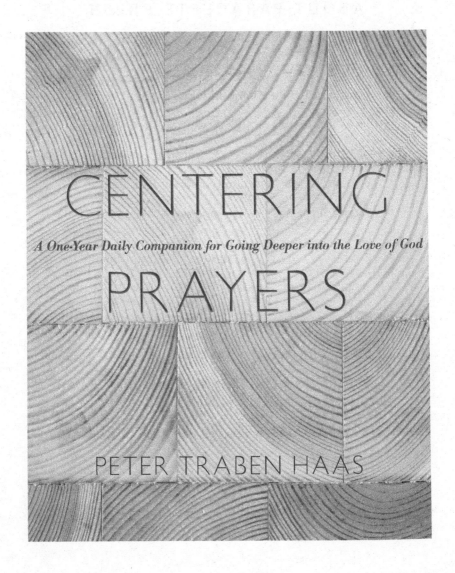